Blue Ribbon Quilts

Linda Causee
Rita Weiss

STERLING

New York / London
www.sterlingpublishing.com

Produced by

CREATIVE PARTNERS LLC

Production Team
Creative Directors: Rita Weiss and
 Jean Leinhauser

Editorial Director: Linda Causee

Photography: Carol Wilson Mansfield

Technical Editing: Ann Harnden

Book Design: Linda Causee

Library of Congress Cataloging-in-Publication Data

Causee, Linda.
 Blue ribbon quilts / Linda Causee & Rita Weiss.
   p. cm.
 Includes index.
 ISBN-13: 978-1-4027-3352-9
 1. Quilting—Patterns. 2. Patchwork--Patterns. I. Weiss, Rita. II. Title.

TT835.C3959654 2008
746.46'041–dc22   2008001962

10 9 8 7 6 5 4 3 2 1

Published by Sterling Publishing Co., Inc.
387 Park Avenue South, New York, NY 10016
© 2008 by The Creative Partners™ LLC
Distributed in Canada by Sterling Publishing
C/o Canadian Manda Group, 165 Dufferin Street
Toronto, Ontario, Canada M6K 3H6
Distributed in the United Kingdom by GMC Distribution Services
Castle Place, 166 High Street, Lewes, East Sussex, England BN7 1XU
Distributed in Australia by Capricorn Link (Australia) Pty. Ltd.
P.O. Box 704, Windsor, NSW 2756, Australia

Printed in China
All rights reserved

Sterling ISBN 978-1-4027-3352-9

For information about custom editions, special sales, premium and corporate purchases, please contact Sterling Special Sales Department at 800-805-5489 or specialsales@sterlingpublishing.com.

Introduction

We sometimes make quilts for our own enjoyment. Occasionally, however, when the last thread has been cut, we are so pleased with our results that we want to share our quilts with everyone.

What better way than to enter a quilt competition! How wonderful to see your quilt hanging with the winners, a bright ribbon proudly pinned beside it.

The quilts in this book have all won prizes in quilt competitions. Some of the competitions were at state fairs, some were fabric challenges sponsored by fabric companies, some were quilt guild contests. No matter what the venue, no matter the prize, it is gratifying to know that someone appreciated the time, the energy and the creativity that went into the making of these quilts.

Lest you think that entering quilt competitions is a modern phenomena, we have included three quilts from the early part of the last century, all of which had won prizes. Perhaps it was the fact that they were prize winners that made their owners keep them and affectionately care for them so that those who inherited these lovely quilts have inherited quilts in pristine condition.

We are grateful to all the quilt owners who have permitted us to share these *Blue Ribbon Quilts*.

Contents

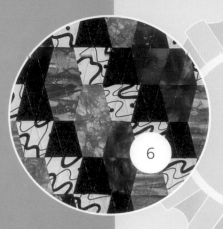

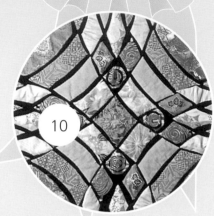

32

72

92

50

78

56

98

84

62

104

The brilliant swirls of color in the challenge fabrics that were hand dyed by Bonny Tinling of Eccentrix Dyeworks provided the inspiration for this one-patch quilt. It won first place in the pieced category of the Eccentrix "Hand-Dyed Textiles Fabric Challenge I for Quilters." Any number of colors can be used for the lamps, as long as they stand out against the lamp bases and the background.

Lava Lamps

by Margrette Carr

Approximate Size
40" x 40"

Materials
Fat quarter each peach, blue, red, purple, pink (lamps)
1 yard black (lamp bases, binding)
1 yard light (background)
2 yards backing
Batting

Pattern
Tumbler (page 9)

Cutting
Blocks
24 Tumblers each, blue, red, purple and pink
22 Tumblers, peach
58 Tumblers, black
58 Tumblers, light

Finishing
5 strips, 3" wide, black (binding)

Margrette Carr fell in love with piecing over ten years ago when she met Pat Yamin of Come Quilt With Me, Inc and discovered that her passion for accuracy could be fulfilled with Pat's acrylic templates. Within a year, she had cut so many tumbler patches from her own and her sister's stashes that there was more than enough for two bed-sized quilts.

Now ten years later she is still cutting, piecing and quilting. Her "Antique Log Cabin Revisited" appeared in *Log Cabin Quilts* published by Sterling Publishing.

While traditional piecing remains her favorite method of quilt construction, Margrette also produces pieces involving other techniques. From her home studio in San Diego, she continues to produce quilts for herself, family, friends, contests and shows.

For another prize-winning quilt by Margrette Carr, see page 50.

Instructions

1. Lay out all the tumblers in a pleasing arrangement of cascading lava lamps. **(Diagram 1)**

Diagram 1

2. Using accurate ¼" seams, piece horizontal rows, pressing seams in each row in opposite direction from the adjacent rows. **(Diagram 2)**

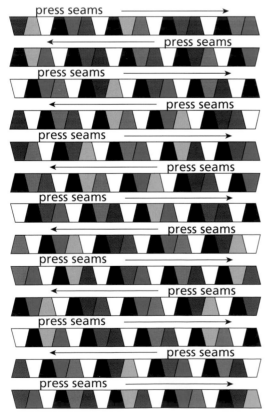

Diagram 2

3. Sew rows together, matching intersections and pressing all seams toward the bottom of the quilt. **(Diagram 3)**

Diagram 3

4. Trim sides straight. **(Diagram 4)**

Diagram 4

5. Refer to Finishing Your Quilt, pages 121 to 127, to complete your quilt.

Note: *The photographed quilt was machine quilted with metallic thread in straight lines following the angles of the tumbler shapes.*

8

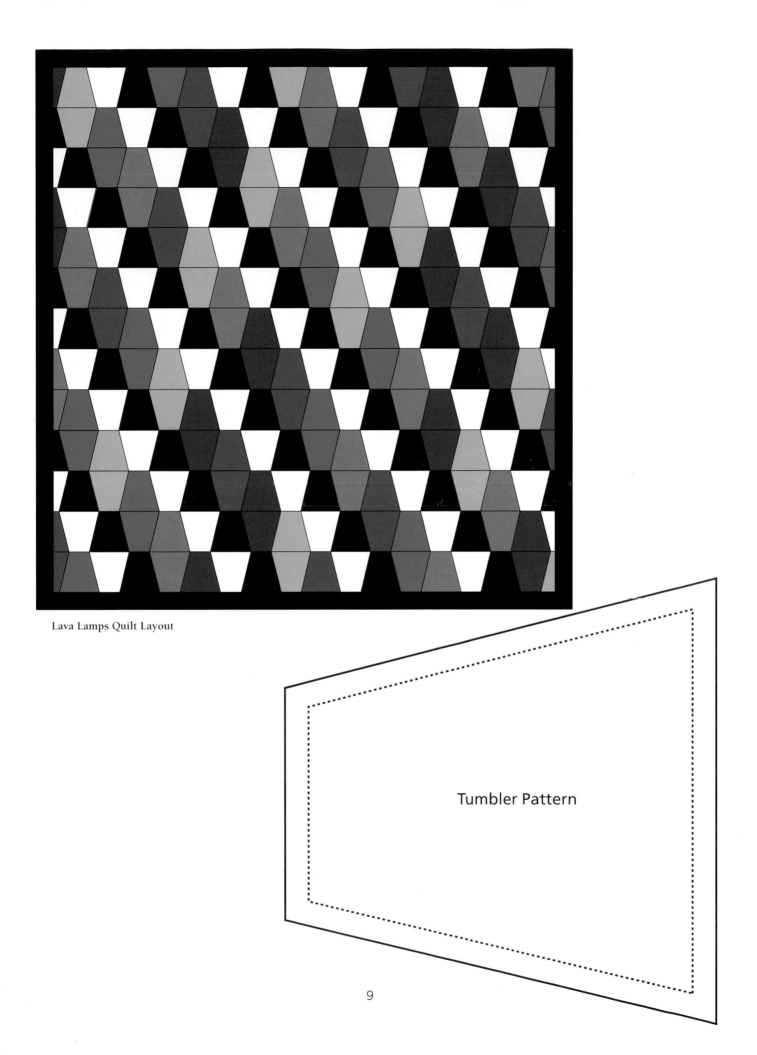

Lava Lamps Quilt Layout

Tumbler Pattern

9

A gift of fabric scraps from a friend who makes lovely Geisha dolls was the impetus for the quiltmaker to create this quilt. She had read and was inspired by the book Quilting with Japanese Fabrics by Kitty Pippen. The quilt is completely hand appliqued and hand quilted. Entered in the 2004 Orange County Fair, it won a ribbon.

Asian Influence

by Ada LeClaire

Approximate Size
41" x 41"

Materials
3 yards black (includes backing and binding)
Assorted scraps of Japanese fabrics
Freezer paper or template plastic for appliqué
Matching thread
Two sheets of mylar (optional)

Patterns
Diagonal Circle Pieces (page 14)
Center Appliqué (page 14)
Horizontal/Vertical Circle Pieces (page 15)
Upper Right Corner Appliqué Pieces (page 16)
Upper Left Corner Appliqué Pieces (page 16)
Lower Left Corner Appliqué Pieces (page 17)
Lower Right Corner Appliqué Pieces (page 17)

Cutting
2 squares, 42" x 42", black (background and backing)
5 strips, 2¹/₂"-wide, black (binding)

A self-taught quilter, Ada LeClair began quilting around 1978 making baby quilts to give as gifts. She learned her techniques from books and maga zines, which in those days insisted that everything had to be done by hand. Ada started out making everything by hand piecing and hand quilting. Eventually she was forced to switch to using the sewing machine in order to complete all of the quilts waiting for her. Ada still likes to make at least one hand-quilted project every year.

Ada's other prize-winning project in this book, "Cottage Door," appears on page 98.

Instructions

1. Make Templates using the patterns on pages 14 to 17. Read the pattern note regarding the Diagonal Circle Pieces.

2. Prepare pattern pieces for appliqué using assorted scraps of Japanese fabrics and referring to Appliqué, pages 112 to 115.

3. Fold one of the 42" black squares in quarters. (**Diagram 1**) Finger press creases.

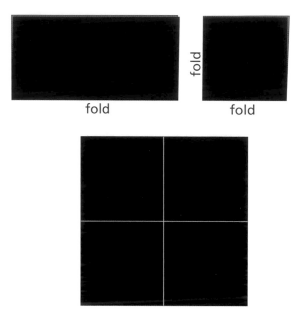

fold   fold

Diagram 1

4. Fold again diagonally. (**Diagram 2**) Finger press creases.

 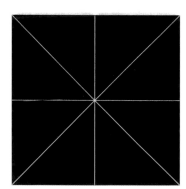

Diagram 2

Hint: *Trace patterns from pages 14 and 15 onto mylar to help with placement of Circle.*

5. Baste Horizontal/Vertical Circle Pieces in place using the horizontal and vertical creases as guidelines. (**Diagram 3**)

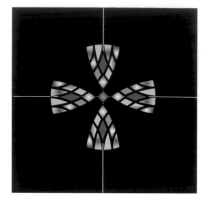

Diagram 3

6. Baste Diagonal Circle Pieces in place along the diagonal creases. (**Diagram 4**)

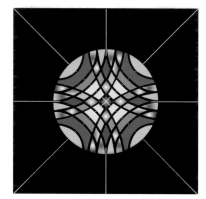

Diagram 4

7. Appliqué pieces to background using matching thread.

8. For Corners, cut motifs from Japanese fabrics or make templates using patterns on pages 16 and 17. Then baste and appliqué in place.

9. Refer to Finishing Your Quilt, pages 121 to 127, to complete your quilt.

Asian Influence Quilt Layout

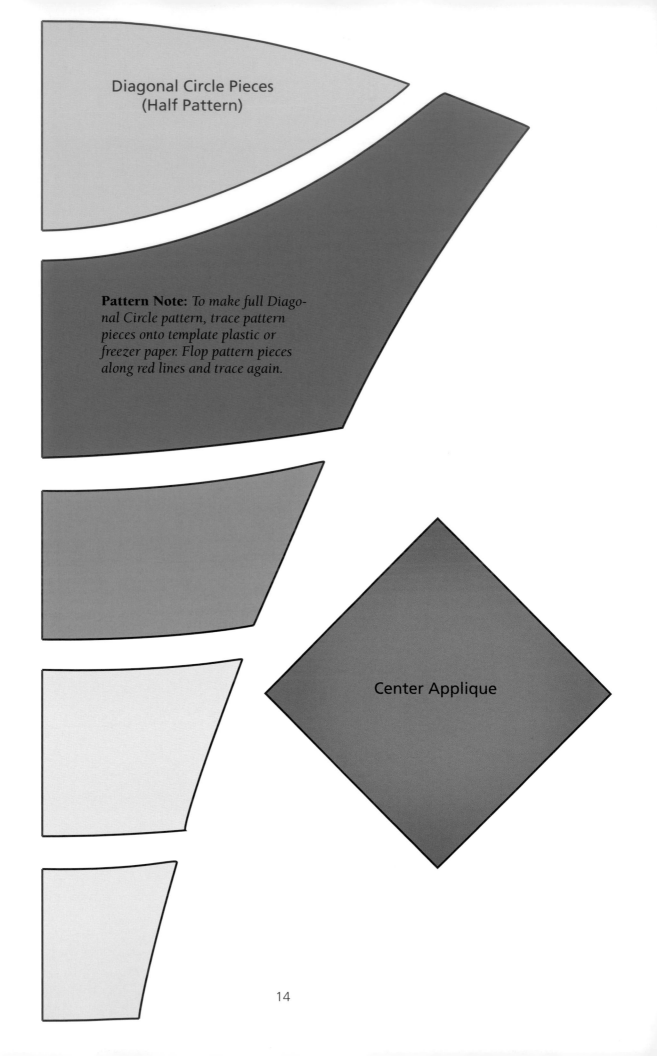

Diagonal Circle Pieces
(Half Pattern)

Pattern Note: *To make full Diagonal Circle pattern, trace pattern
pieces onto template plastic or
freezer paper. Flop pattern pieces
along red lines and trace again.*

Center Applique

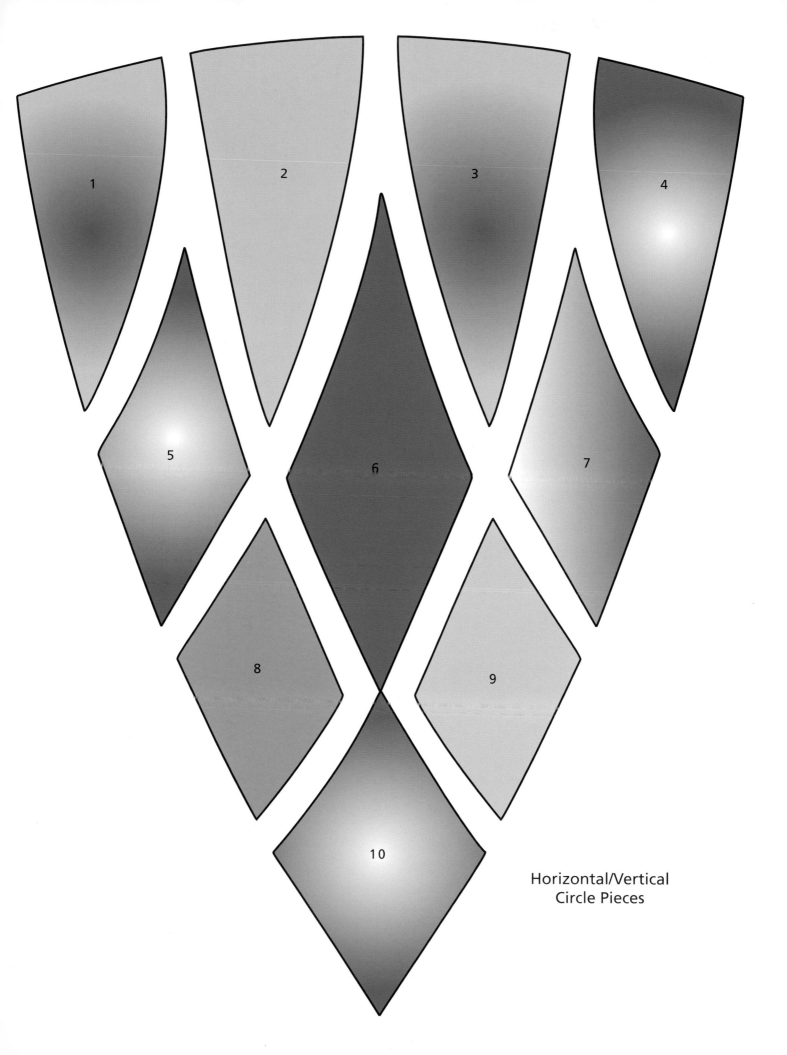

Horizontal/Vertical
Circle Pieces

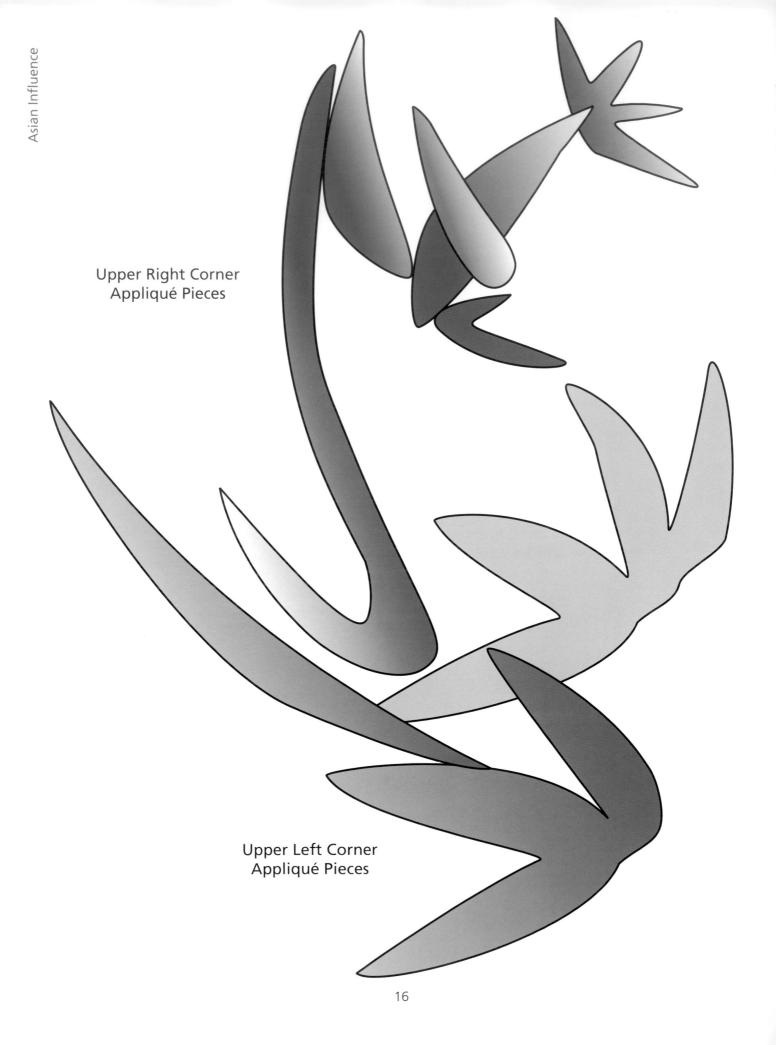

Upper Right Corner
Appliqué Pieces

Upper Left Corner
Appliqué Pieces

16

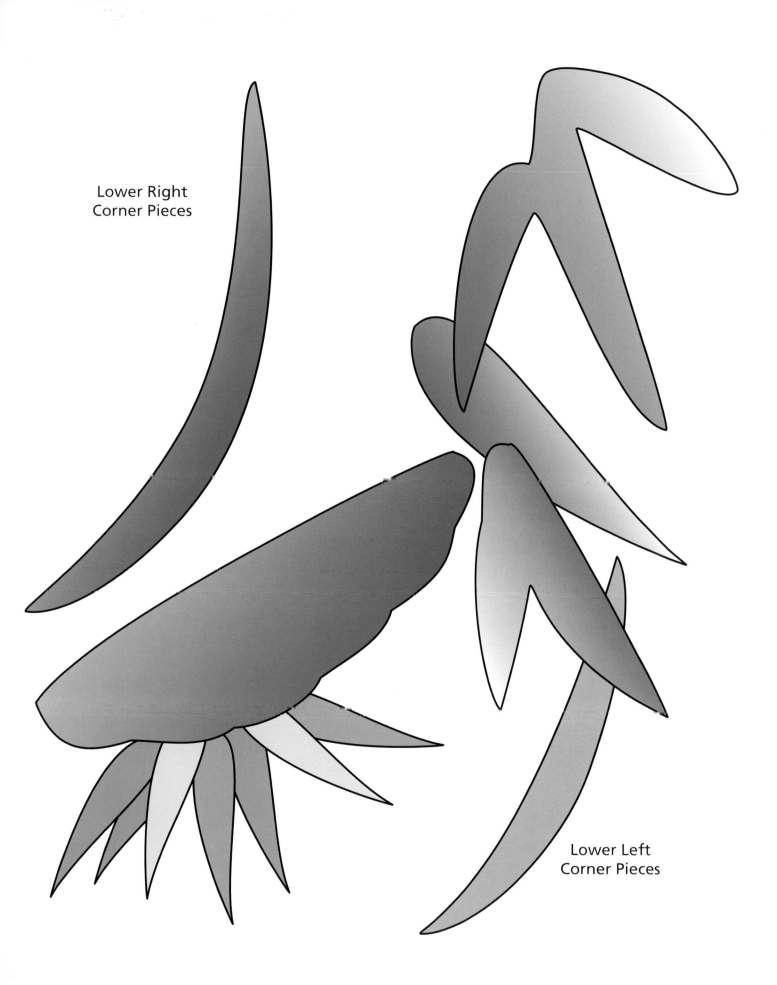

Lower Right
Corner Pieces

Lower Left
Corner Pieces

This exquisite Lily of the Valley quilt was made in 1934 as a wedding gift for the quilter's brother and his new wife. Before delivering the gift, the quilter entered the quilt in the local county fair where it won a first place ribbon, enhancing the glamour of the present. The Lily of the Valley design is not only in the beautifully executed appliques but appears again as quilting stitches in the plain blocks.

Lily of the Valley

by Marian Wilson Beard

Approximate Size

70" x 88"

Materials

5 yards light green
3 yards dark green (includes sashing, border and binding)
½ yard white
5¼ yards backing
Batting
5 sheets of copy paper and tape
Flat head pins (optional)
1 sheet of mylar
1 sheet of template plastic
Removable fabric marking pen or pencil

Patterns

Quarter Diamond (page 22)
Lily of the Valley (page 24)
Lily of the Valley Quilting Pattern (page 25)

Note: *Make a pattern for the Large Diamond by cutting a paper rectangle, 8¼" x 10½". Draw a line from one corner to the opposite corner. (**Diagram A**) Cut out along drawn line. Repeat. Lay the four resulting triangles on a flat surface forming a Large Diamond. Tape together to complete Large Diamond pattern. (**Diagram B**)*

Diagram A

Diagram B

Marian Wilson Beard was born in Warren, Illinois in 1903. After graduating from Warren High School she immediately began teaching in the local school. She left teaching after two years and enrolled in the De Kalb Normal School, which is now Northern Illinois University.

It was there that she met and married Roy Beard. For the next 11 years, the Beards tried unsuccessfully to have a family. That Marion loved children is documented by the fact that the Beards took in poor children from Chicago for whole summers—fed them, clothed them and gave them a new chance in life.

Less than a year after completing this quilt, Marian died. She had finally succeeded in becoming pregnant, but unfortunately the pregnancy was an ectopic one that was fatal in those days.

Marian's brother and his wife kept the quilt in pristine condition and when they died, left this beautiful example of a blue ribbon quilt to their daughter.

Cut remaining three sheets to 8¼" x 10½". Draw diagonal line and cut along line. Tape two pieces together to make a Horizontal Half Diamond; tape two pieces together to make Vertical Half Diamond. Remaining triangles are Corner Diamond patterns. (**Diagram C**)

Diagram C

Cutting

Note: *Refer to Appliqué, pages 112 to 115, to prepare Lily of the Valley flowers for 16 blocks. Use dark green for Stems and Leaves and white for Flowers.*

*25 Large Diamonds, light green
*6 Vertical Half Diamonds, light green
*6 Horizontal Half Diamonds, light green
*4 Corner Diamonds, light green
22 strips, 1¼"-wide strips, dark green (sashing)
9 strips, 2½"-wide, dark green (border)
9 strips, 2½"-wide, dark green (binding

*See steps 1 to 3 in Instructions below before cutting Diamonds.

Instructions

Making the Blocks

1. Fold length of light green fabric in half lengthwise, matching selvages. Cut out Large Diamonds, Vertical Half Diamonds, Horizontal Half Diamonds and Corner Diamonds from light green fabric. (**Diagram 1**)

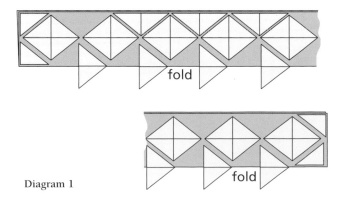

Diagram 1

2. Place folded fabric on cutting mat. Position Large Diamond pattern on fabric; pin pattern to fabric using flat head pins. Place acrylic ruler on pattern with edge of ruler ¼" beyond one of the pattern edges and cut with a rotary cutter. (**Diagram 2**) Move the ruler along each of the remaining edges and cut out ¼" beyond pattern edges for seam allowance.

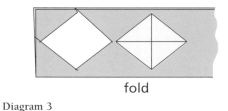

fold

Diagram 2

3. Move pattern at least 1½" away from point of previous Large Diamond and cut another Diamond. (**Diagram 3**) Repeat until you have 25 Large Diamonds.

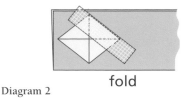

fold

Diagram 3

4. Cut out remaining background pieces – six Vertical Half Diamonds, six Horizontal Half Diamonds, and four Corner Diamonds.

5. Trace the entire Lily of the Valley pattern onto a sheet of mylar. Use this for placement of the appliqué onto the light green Large Diamonds.

6. Position appliqué pieces onto a Large Diamond and pin in place. Hand appliqué in place. (**Diagram 4**) Repeat for a total of 16 Lily of the Valley Diamonds.

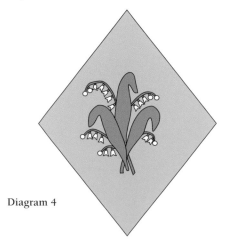

Diagram 4

Finishing the Quilt

1. Place Lily of the Valley Diamonds in four rows of four. Fill in with plain Diamonds. Place Vertical Half Diamonds along sides and Horizontal Half Diamonds along top and bottom; place Corner Diamonds in the corners. (**Diagram 5**)

Diagram 5

2. Sew the Diamonds together in diagonal rows then sew rows together. (**Diagram 6**)

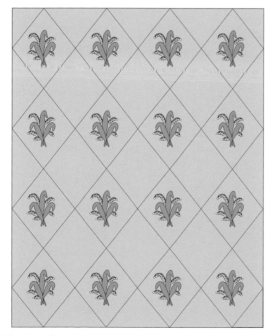

Diagram 6

3. Sew 1¼"-wide sashing strips end to end using a diagonal seam. Trim ¼" from stitching and press seam open. (**Diagram 7**)

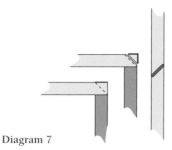

Diagram 7

4. Place strip centered over a diagonal seam; cut off. Center strip over another seam and cut off. Continue placing strip and cutting until all diagonal seams in one direction are covered. (**Diagram 8**)

Diagram 8

5. Press long edges of each cut strip under ¼". Center folded strip over seam line and hand appliqué in place.

6. Repeat steps 4 and 5 for seams going in the other direction. (**Diagram 9**)

Diagram 9

7. Measure quilt top lengthwise. Piece and cut 2½"-wide dark green strips to that length. Sew to sides of quilt top. Measure quilt top crosswise. Piece and cut 2½"-wide dark green strips to that length. Sew to top and bottom of quilt top.

8. Trace Lily of the Valley quilting pattern onto template plastic and cut out. Trace pattern onto plain Large Diamonds.

9. Refer to Finishing Your Quilt, pages 121 to 127, to complete your quilt.

Quarter Diamond

Lily of the Valley Quilt Layout

Lily of the Valley
Appliqué Pattern

24

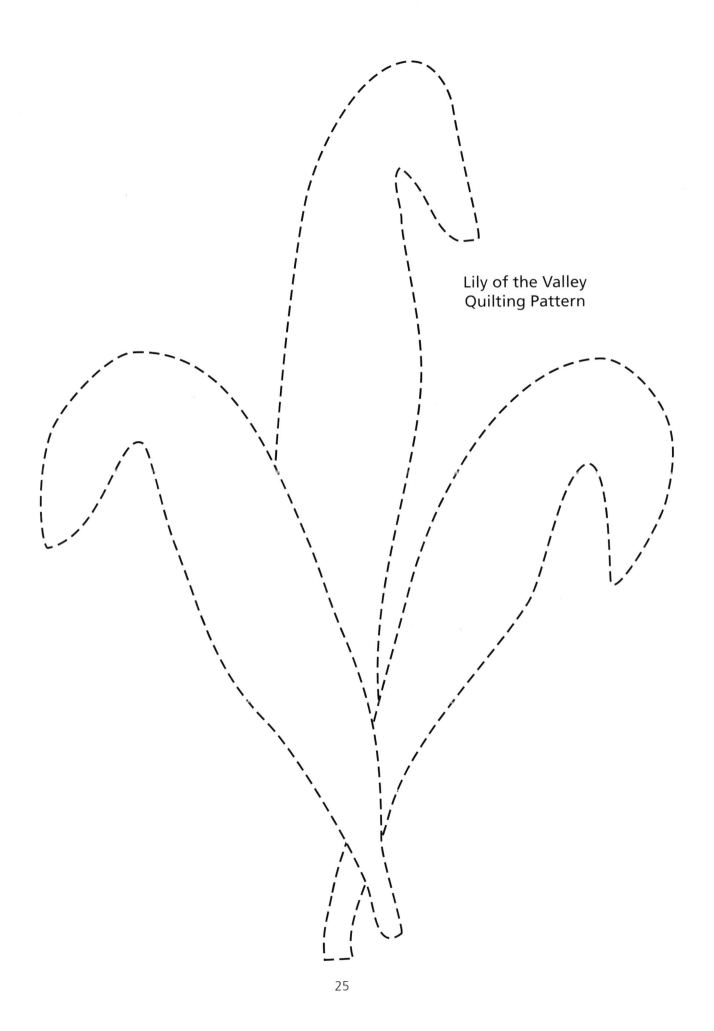

Lily of the Valley
Quilting Pattern

25

Inspired by a class called "Strips 'n Curves" given by Louisa Smith, the quiltmaker created this fascinating quilt which was displayed at the San Diego Quilt Show and later won a ribbon at the San Diego County Fair in 2005. In 2006, the quilt was juried into the prestigious International Quilt Festival competition.

Easy Road

By Sandy Thompson

Approximate Size
44" x 62"

Materials
24 fat quarters of assorted batiks
1 yard purple batik (first border, binding)
2¾ yards backing
Batting
Template plastic
Fabric marking pencil

Pattern
Drunkard's Path A and B (page 31)

Cutting
Blocks
12 strips, 1½"-wide, batik fat quarters (Cut strips along the 22" length of all but 2 fat quarters.)

Finishing
5 strips, 1½"-wide, purple batik (first border)
6 strips, 2½"-wide, purple batik (binding)

Sandy Thompson's parents were artists who encouraged their children to do all kinds of craft projects, including sewing which Sandy did from the time she was seven.

After graduating from college, Sandy joined a manufacturing company that produced a full line of baby bedding: quilts, bumpers, canopies, etc. This is where Sandy learned to make quilts the fastest and easiest way possible.

Although today Sandy loves the whole process of quiltmaking, she doesn't like to fuss over any quilt. She does, however, admire those who love to make quilts by hand. But for her, she loves to find the easiest way to make a pattern work. Machine quilting appeals to her creative senses.

Sandy has been a quilt teacher for the past 14 years, especially enjoying her work with new quilters and sharing their excitement as they learn new techniques.

Instructions

1. Refer to Templates, page 120, and make templates from template plastic using patterns on page 31.

2. Sew 1½"-wide strips together.

Note: *Sew strips in groups of 14 for easier handling. Make some strip sets with mostly light batiks and some with mostly darks.* (**Diagram 1**)

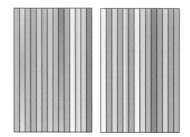

Diagram 1

3. Place template A on a strip set and trace using a fabric marking pen or pencil. Be sure to mark midpoints on each piece. You can get three template A on each strip set. You will need a total of 22 A. (**Diagram 2**) Cut pieces along drawn lines.

Diagram 2

4. Place template B on a strip set and trace using a fabric marking pen or pencil. Be sure to mark midpoints on each piece. You can get three template B on each strip set. You will need a total of 21 B. (**Diagram 3**) Cut pieces along drawn lines.

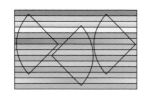

Diagram 3

5. Trace and cut three A and two B from remaining fat quarters. (**Diagram 4**)

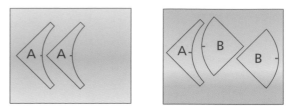

Diagram 4

6. Refer to Curved Piecing, pages 120 to 121, to sew striped A and B pieces. (**Diagram 5**) Sew dark A's to light B's and light A's to dark B's. Make a total of 19 striped blocks.

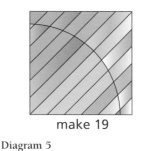

make 19

Diagram 5

7. Sew a solid A to a striped B. Repeat. (**Diagram 6**)

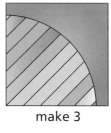

make 3

Diagram 6

8. Sew a striped A to a solid B. Repeat two more times. (**Diagram 7**)

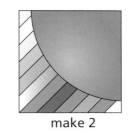

make 2

Diagram 7

9. Place blocks in six rows of four blocks. (**Diagram 8**)

Note: *Arrange blocks referring to Diagram or until you have your own pleasing arrangement.*

Diagram 8

10. Sew blocks together in rows; press seams for rows in alternating directions. Sew rows together.

11. Cut out four circles from remaining batik scraps. Referring to Appliqué, pages 112 to 115, appliqué in place on quilt top. (**Diagram 9**)

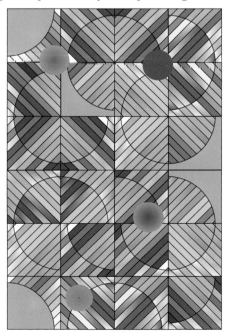

Diagram 9

12. Measure quilt top lengthwise; cut two 1½"-wide purple batik strips to that length. Sew to sides of quilt. Press seams toward border.

13. Measure quilt top crosswise; cut two 1½"-wide purple batik strips to that length. Sew to top and bottom of quilt. Press seams toward border.

14. For pieced border, cut 4"-wide strips at a 45-degree angle from remaining strip sets. (**Diagram 10**)

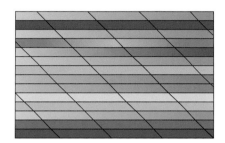

Diagram 10

15. Place quilt top on a flat surface and position strip sections along all four sides until desired placement is achieved.

16. Sew strip sections together to make the four border strips. Place strip sections right sides together, offsetting the strips ¼"; sew. (**Diagram 11**)

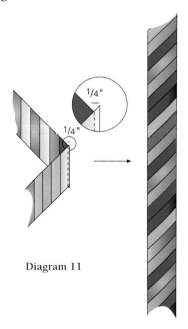

Diagram 11

Note: *The pieced border in the photographed quilt is sewn in sections that are going in different directions. There are also solid (not striped) sections in the upper and lower left corners and right side border. To simplify the border, sew strips in the same direction.* (**Diagram 12**)

Diagram 12

17. Sew borders to the quilt. Be sure border strips are long enough for mitering. See Mitered Borders, pages 121 to 122.

18. Refer to Finishing Your Quilt, pages 121 to 127, to complete your quilt.

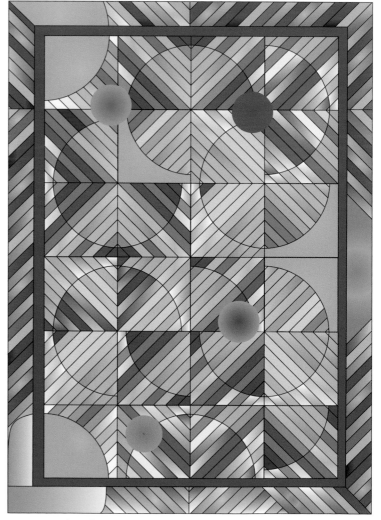

Easy Road Quilt Layout

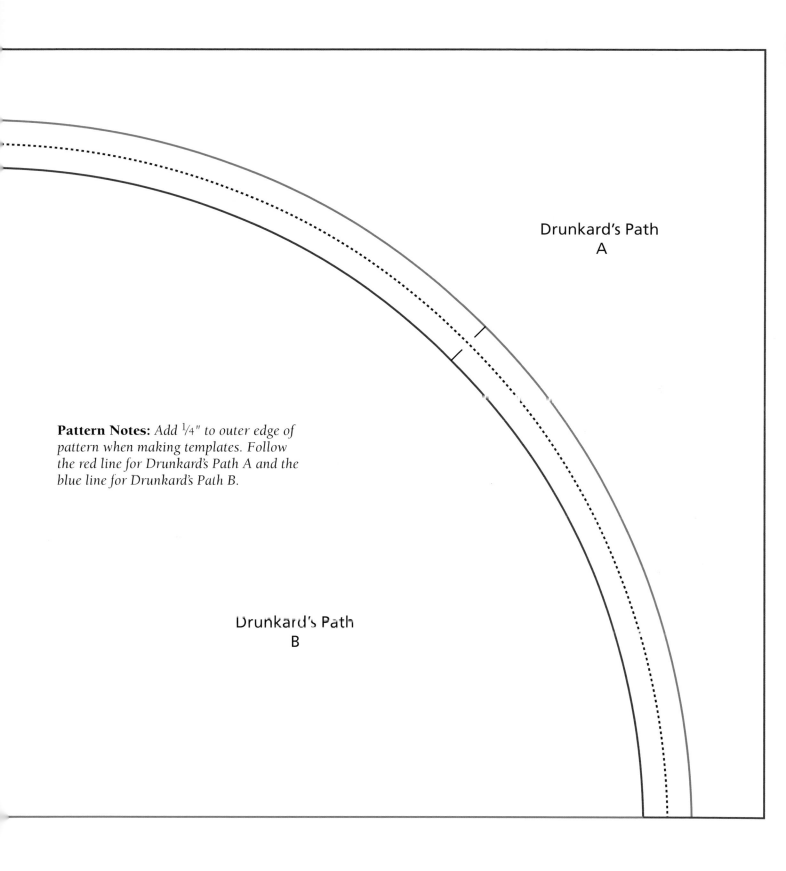

Drunkard's Path
A

Pattern Notes: *Add ¼" to outer edge of pattern when making templates. Follow the red line for Drunkard's Path A and the blue line for Drunkard's Path B.*

Drunkard's Path
B

A lover of orchids, the quiltmaker chose to honor the flower by creating this quilt. She drew the orchids, dyed the fabrics, and appliquéd the flowers onto the white background. Where necessary, she added embroidery to enhance the designs. Entered in several quilt shows in Colorado, the quilt won a Best of Show as well as several other awards.

Through My Garden Window

by Afton Barnes

Approximate Size
82" x 82"

Block Size
16" x 16" finished

Materials
6½ yards white, muslin or light background
1 yard light pink
1 yard medium pink
1 yard dark pink
Fat quarters of light and dark purple, light, medium and dark green, gray, yellow
5 yards backing
Batting
Template plastic or freezer paper
Erasable fabric pen or pencil
Gold, rosy pink, green, black, white embroidery floss
White fabric paint

Patterns
Note: *Enlarge all patterns listed below 200% to make the bed-size quilt shown on the opposite page. To make a wall hanging that measures 41" x 41", use patterns as is and cut yardage requirements in half.*

Orchid Basket A (page 38)
Orchid Basket B (page 39)
Orchid Wreath (page 40)
Heart Wreath (page 41)
Orchid Swag (page 42)
Corner Scallop with Orchid (page 43)
Side Border Scallop with Orchid (page 44)
Orchid 1 Quilting Pattern (page 45)
Orchid 2 Quilting Pattern (page 46)
Orchid 3 Quilting Pattern (page 47)
Orchid 4 Quilting Pattern (page 48)
Border Orchid Quilting Pattern (page 49)

Kay Quella is the proud owner of this beautiful quilt which was made by her mother, Afton Barnes.

For many years, Afton raised orchids in a greenhouse attached to her house that her husband had built. There were over 200 orchids in this greenhouse.

In addition to being a gardener, Afton was a painter and a quilter.

When she was 73, she decided to honor her orchids forever by making a quilt and doing an oil painting of the flowers.

Today both the quilt and the oil painting are cherished by Afton's daughter, Kay Quella.

There are many different varieties of orchids in the quilt, each of which Afton painstakingly drew to create her appliqué and quilting patterns. The entire quilt was made and quilted by hand and completed in a year.

Cutting

Bed quilt

- 5 squares, 17" x 17", white
- 4 squares, 16½" x 16½", white
- 2 strips, 18" x 48½", white
- 2 strips, 18" x 82½", white
- 8 strips, 2½"-wide, binding (**Note:** *Make bias strips, page 124, if making scalloped edges.*)

Wallhanging

- 5 squares, 9" x 9", white
- 4 squares, 8½" x 8½", white
- 2 strips, 9" x 24½", white
- 2 strips, 9" x 41½", white
- 5 strips, 2½"-wide, binding

Instructions

Appliquéing the Blocks and Borders

1. Read Appliqué, pages 112 to 115, and prepare appliqué pieces for blocks.

Hint: *To keep appliqué organized, place pieces for a single block in a recloseable baggie.*

2. Starting with one of the blocks, appliqué pieces to 17" white square. Continue appliquéing until all blocks are finished. (**Diagram 1**) Trim blocks to 16½" square.

Diagram 1

Note: *See individual patterns for embroidery notes to finish blocks.*

3. Prepare 12 Side Border Scallops from dark pink fabric, 12 from medium pink and 12 from light pink. For Side Borders, find center of 18" x 48½" white strip. Position the center of a dark pink Scallop on the center of the white strip, about 8" from one long edge. Appliqué lower edge in place. (**Diagram 2**)

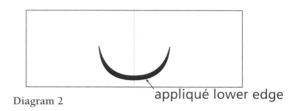

Diagram 2   appliqué lower edge

4. Appliqué a dark pink Scallop on each side of center Scallop. The Scallops should end about ¼" to ½" from edge of strip. (**Diagram 3**)

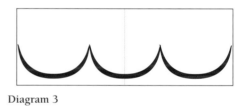

Diagram 3

5. Position medium pink Scallops with folded lower edge overlapping dark pink Scallops and appliqué lower edges in place. (**Diagram 4**)

Diagram 4

6. Appliqué lower edges of light pink Scallops onto medium pink Scallops. Finish by appliquéing upper edge to background. (**Diagram 5**)

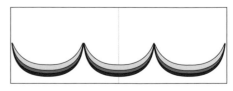

Diagram 5

7. Repeat steps 3 to 5 for remaining 18" x 48½" white strip.

8. For top and bottom borders, find center of 18" x 82½" white strip. Position the center of a dark pink Scallop on the center of the white strip, about 4" from one long edge. Appliqué lower edge in place. Appliqué a dark pink Scallop on each side of center Scallop.

9. Position medium pink Scallops with folded lower edge overlapping dark pink Scallops and appliqué lower edges in place.

10. Appliqué lower edges of light pink Scallops onto medium pink Scallops; appliqué upper edge. (**Diagram 6**)

Diagram 6

11. Prepare for appliqué, four Corner Scallops from dark pink fabric, four from medium pink and four from light pink. Position dark pink Corner Scallop on white strip and appliqué in place. (**Diagram 7**)

Diagram 7

Hint: *To be sure that Corner Scallop will match up with end Scallop of the adjacent 18" x 48½" white strip, place the strips next to each other on a flat surface. Adjust Corner Scallop so that it will meet up with end Scallop when strips are sewn together.* (**Diagram 8**)

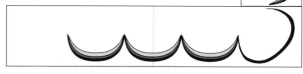

Diagram 8

12. Appliqué medium pink and light pink Corner Scallops in place. (**Diagram 9**)

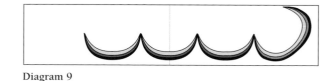

Diagram 9

13. Repeat steps 11 and 12 on other end of strip. (**Diagram 10**) Repeat for remaining 18" x 82½" white strip.

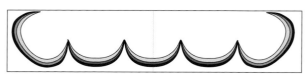

Diagram 10

14. Appliqué Border Orchid at each Scallop point. (**Diagram 11**)

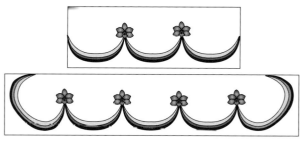

Diagram 11

15. Appliqué Corner Orchids inside Corner Scallops. (**Diagram 12**)

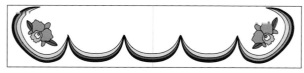

Diagram 12

Putting the Quilt Together

1. Place Appliqué blocks alternating with 16½" squares in three rows of three blocks. Sew blocks together in rows then sew rows together.

2. Sew 18" x 48½" appliquéd border strip to each side of quilt top. Sew 18" x 82½" appliquéd border strips to top and bottom of quilt.

3. Appliqué remaining Border Orchids at corners. (**Diagram 13**)

Diagram 13

4. Using an erasable fabric pen or pencil, trace all quilting patterns (pages 45 to 49) onto 16½" white squares and inside each Border Scallop.

5. Refer to Finishing Your Quilt, pages 121 to 127, to layer and quilt your quilt. Trim edge of quilted quilt to follow curves of dark pink Scallop. (**Diagram 14**)

Diagram 14

6. Make bias binding and add referring to Attaching Continuous Machine Binding, page 125 to 126.

Embroidery Stitches

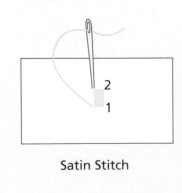

Satin Stitch

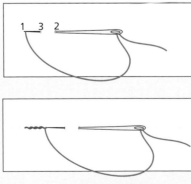

Stem Stitch

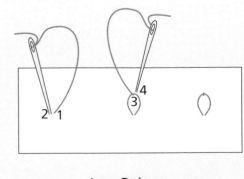

Lazy Daisy

Through My Garden Window Quilt Layout

Note: *Be sure to enlarge all patterns on pages 38 to 49 to 200% to make the bed-size quilt shown on page 32.*

Orchid Basket A

Finishing Notes: *See Embroidery Stitches, page 36.*

For gold areas of flowers, embroider using the Satin Stitch and 2 to 3 strands of gold emboidery floss.

For thin white lines, use white fabric paint and a thin paint brush; or embroider using the Stem Stitch and 2 to 3 strands of white embroidery floss for highlights on the flowers.

For white flower centers, embroider using the Satin Stitch and 2 to 3 strands of white embroidery floss.

For veins in leaves, embroider using the Stem Stitch and 2 to 3 strands of green embroidery floss.

Orchid Basket B

Finishing Notes: *See Embroidery Stitches, page 36.*

For white edges of flowers, use white paint and a thin paint brush; or embroider using the Stem Stitch and 2 to 3 strands of white embriodery floss.

For white flower centers, embroider using the Satin Stitch and 2 to 3 strands of white embroidery floss.

For veins in leaves and black highlights, embroider using the Stem Stitch and 2 to 3 strands of black embroidery floss.

Orchid Wreath

Finishing Notes: *See Embroidery Stitches, page 36.*

For gold centers of flowers, embroider using the Satin Stitch and 2 to 3 strands of gold emboidery floss.

For white flower centers, embroider using the Satin Stitch and 2 to 3 strands of white embroidery floss.

For veins in leaves, and stems, embroider using the Stem Stitch and 2 to 3 strands of black embroidery floss.

For pink curly lines, embroidery using Stem Stitch and 2 to 3 strands of rosy pink floss.

Heart Wreath

Finishing Notes: *See Embroidery Stitches, page 36.*

For short pink lines on flowers, embroider using the Straight Stitch and 2 to 3 strands of rosy pink embroidery floss.

For vine, embroider using the Stem Stitch and 2 to 3 strands of green embroidery floss.

For vine leaves, embroider using the Lazy Daisy stitch and 2 to 3 stands of green embroidery floss.

Orchid Swag

Finishing Notes: *See Embroidery Stitches, page 36.*

For pink flower highlights, embroider using Stem Stitch and 2 to 3 strands of rosy pink embroidery floss.

For black flower highlights, embroider using Stem Stitch and 2 to 3 strands of black embroidery floss.

For white flower centers, embroider using the Satin Stitch and 2 to 3 strands of white embroidery floss.

For veins in leaves, embroider using the Stem Stitch and 2 to 3 strands of black embroidery floss.

For little white circle highlights, use white paint and a thin paint brush.

Corner Scallop with Orchid

Side Border Scallop
with Orchid

Orchid 1 Quilting Pattern

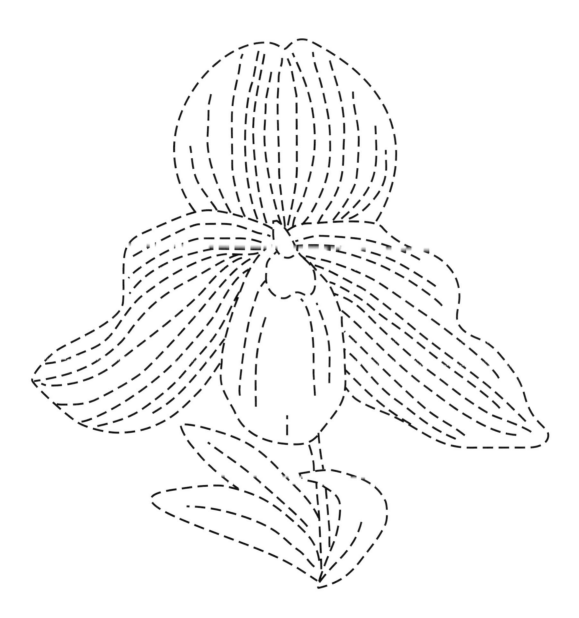

Orchid 2 Quilting Pattern

Orchid 3 Quilting Pattern

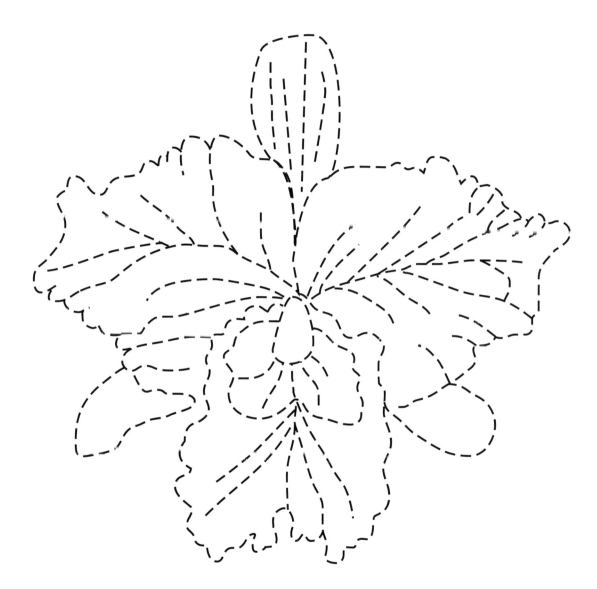

Orchid 4 Quilting Pattern

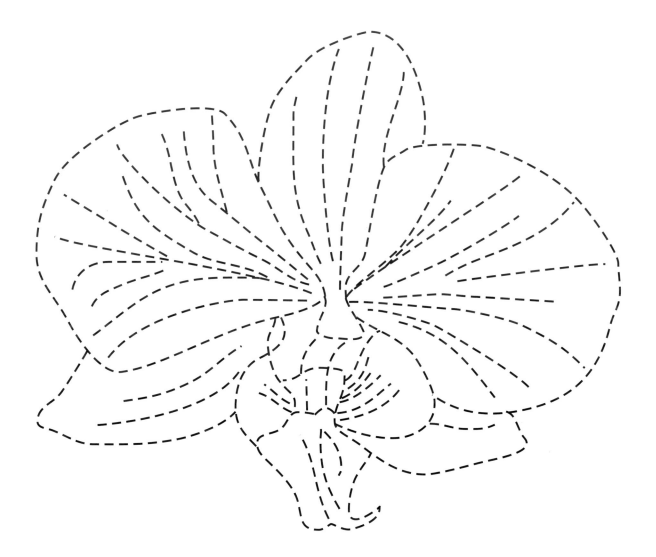

Border Quilting Pattern

This intriguing quilt, made up of both pieced and appliquéd blocks, is embellished with mirrors, sequins and embroidery. Inspired by traditional "ralli" quilts of the Punjab and Sindh provinces of Pakistan, it was the Best of Show winner in the "Eccentrix Dyeworks Fabric Challenge II for Quilters."

Punjab Reflections
by Margrette Carr

Approximate Size
36" x 36"

Materials
1½ yards hand-dyed dark multi-colored fabric (includes binding)
1 yard hand-dyed red fabric
5 fat quarters hand-dyed light fabrics
1½ yards backing
Batting
12 shisha mirrors
Sequins, green, red, gold, and blue
Pearl cotton, black

Pattern
Appliqué X (page 55)

Cutting
Variable Star Blocks
15 squares, 3" x 3", red fabric
10 squares, 3" x 3", dark multi-colored fabric
10 squares, 3¾" x 3¾", dark multi-colored fabric (cut diagonally into quarters for a total of 40 triangles)
10 squares, 3¾" x 3¾", light fabric (cut diagonally into quarters for a total of 40 triangles)

Appliqué Blocks
4 squares, 6" x 6", light fabric (background)
2 squares, 5" x 5", dark multi-colored fabric (Appliqué X)
2 squares, 5" x 5", red (Appliqué X)
8 strips, 1½" x 6", light fabric
8 strips, 1½" x 8", light fabric

In this quilt, Margrette Carr combines traditional patchwork with hand appliqué, embroidery and embellishments to interpret the exotic and highly decorative quilted textiles of Southern Pakistan and Northern India.

Margrette first viewed an exhibit of these remarkable quilts at the International Quilt Festival in Houston in November, 2003. This led to a study of "Ralli" quilts and encouraged her to make this one. Most of these "ralli" quilts are much larger and are used as bed, floor, and table coverings or are suspended from ropes and poles to serve as fans, canopies and tent walls. Smaller "ralli" such as this quilt are used as baby blankets or prayer rugs. Some are folded and sewn into bags to hold wedding gifts, books, or—in the case of snake charmers—serpents.

Margrette spent 20 years "seeing the world" as a Naval officer, but she is now retired and settled in her home with her husband, two cats and lots of quilt fabric. Her other prize-winning quilt, "Lava Lamps", appears on page 6.

Finishing

- 2 strips, 1½" x 22½", dark multi-colored fabric (first border)
- 2 strips, 1½" x 24½", dark multi-colored fabric (first border)
- 2 strips, 2½" x 32", dark multi-colored fabric (third border)
- 2 strips, 2½" x 36½", dark multi-colored fabric (third border)
- 16 squares, 3" x 3", red (pieced border)
- 16 squares, 3" x 3", dark multi-colored fabric (pieced border)
- 15 squares, 4¾" x 4¾", light hand-dyed fabric cut diagonally into quarters for 56 triangles (pieced border)
- 4 squares, 2⅝" x 2⅝", light hand-dyed fabrics cut diagonally in half for 16 triangles (pieced border)
- 4 strips, 3"-wide, dark multi-colored fabric (binding)

Instructions

Variable Star Blocks

1. Place a light and dark triangle right sides together; sew along one short side. (**Diagram 1**) Press seam toward dark triangle. Repeat seven more times.

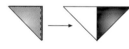

Diagram 1

2. Chain piece triangles to speed up the sewing process; clip threads between pairs. (**Diagram 2**)

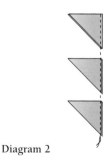

Diagram 2

3. Sew pairs of pieced triangles to make pieced squares. (**Diagram 3**) Press seams open.

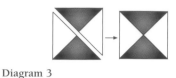

Diagram 3

4. For rows 1 and 3, sew a 3" red and a 3" dark multi-colored square to opposite sides of a pieced square. (**Diagram 4**) Press seams toward solid squares.

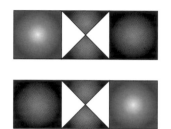

Diagram 4

5. For row 2, sew a pieced square to opposite sides of a 3" red square. (**Diagram 5**) Press seams toward solid square.

Diagram 5

6. Sew rows 1, 2 and 3 together to complete Variable Star block. (**Diagram 6**) Make a total of five Variable Star blocks.

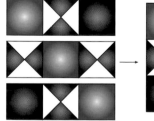
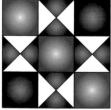

Diagram 6

Appliqué Blocks

1. Cut Appliqué X patterns from the two 5" x 5" red squares and the two 5" x 5" dark multi-colored squares. Prepare the pieces for appliqué referring to Appliqué, pages 112 to 115.

2. Fold 6" x 6" light background squares in quarters and finger press. Using the creases as guidelines, center a dark multi-colored Appliqué X on light background square and baste; repeat with red Appliqué X. (**Diagram 7**)

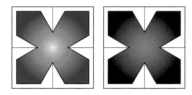

Diagram 7

3. Turning under a ¼" edge all around, secure the appliqué with a blind stitch. Remove the basting stitches.

4. Attach 1½" x 6" strips on opposite sides, and 1½" x 8" strips on top and bottom. (**Diagram 8**) Make two red and two dark multi-colored Appliqué X blocks.

Diagram 8

Making the Quilt

1. Sew Variable Star and Appliqué blocks together in three rows of three blocks to finish center portion of quilt. (**Diagram 9**)

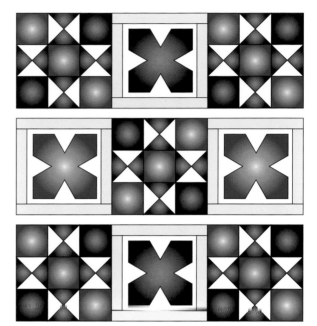

Diagram 9

2. Attach 1½" x 22½" dark multi-colored strips to center. Then sew 1½" x 24½" dark multi-colored strips to top and bottom. (**Diagram 10**)

Diagram 10

3. For pieced side borders, use three red and four dark 3" squares connected by 12 light quarter-square triangles; add a small light half-square triangle at each end. (**Diagram 11**) Attach to sides.

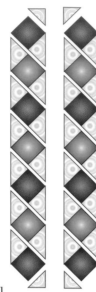

Diagram 11

4. Construct each top and bottom pieced border unit using three red and four dark 3" squares connected by 14 light quarter-square triangles. (**Diagram 12**) Attach to top and bottom.

Diagram 12

5. To make pieced border corners, sew light quarter-square triangles to two opposite sides of red 3" squares; sew light half-square triangle on third side. Sew a completed pieced border corner to each corner. (**Diagram 13**)

Diagram 13

6. Sew 2½" x 32" dark multi-colored strips to sides of quilt. Press seams. Sew 2½" x 36½" dark multi-colored strips to top and bottom.

7. Refer to Finishing Your Quilt, pages 121 to 127 to baste and quilt as desired. Attach continuous binding using the 3"-wide dark multi-colored strips.

Note: *The photographed quilt was machine quilted with hand-dyed pearl cotton in the bobbin and two strands of variegated machine embroidery thread through the needle. Most of the quilting was done from the back.*

8. Referring to photograph, attach a mirror in the center of each appliqué block and the centers of random border squares using pearl cotton. Sew sequins by hand using hand-dyed pearl cotton.

Punjab Reflections Quilt Layout

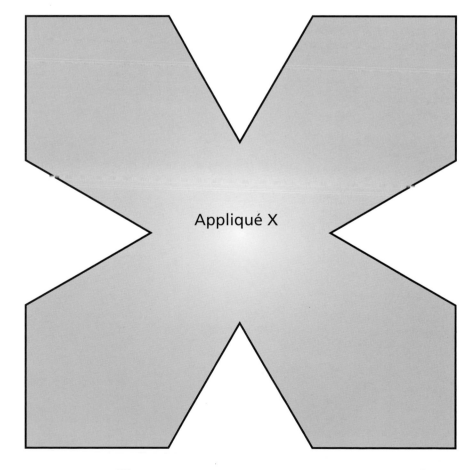

Appliqué X

Over thirty years ago when the quilter was expecting her first child, she made a puppy quilt similar to this one. Not knowing anything about quilting, she used cotton/polyester blends and did a small zigzag around the pieces. The quilt still survives today despite numerous washings. She recreated the pattern and the quilt using modern methods and hand stitching. All of the puppies in this contemporary version are wearing make-up! She used acrylic paint and put a highlight in each eye. Some of the ears have been lightly painted with diluted acrylic paint to give them more contrast. The quilt won a ribbon in the professional division at the county fair.

Puppy Love

by Pamela Kay

Approximate Size

40" x 52"

Materials

1 yard light tan (appliqué background)
1¼ yards assorted brown and rust prints (sashing)
⅝ yard assorted tan and light brown prints (squares)
Assorted brown, beige and tan print and solid scraps (appliqué)
Scrap black (appliqué)
¼ yard rust print (first border)
1 yard dark brown print (second border and binding)
1¾ yards backing
Batting
Template plastic or freezer paper
Fabric marking pencil

Patterns

Puppy (page 61)

Cutting

Blocks/Sashing

12 squares, 10" x 10", light tan (background)
48 strips, 1¾" x 9½", assorted brown and rust prints (sashing strips)
96 squares, 1¾" x 1¾", assorted tan and light brown prints (sashing squares)
48 squares, 2⅛ x 2⅛", assorted tan and light brown prints (triangle squares)

Finishing

5 strips, 1"-wide, rust print (first border)
5 strips, 3"-wide, dark brown print (second border)
5 strips, 2½"-wide, dark brown print (binding)

Twenty years ago, Pam Kay, who had been quilting in earnest for a year, started working at her local quilt shop. She took every quilt class offered by the shop and worked in all mediums. She soon discovered her favorite style was the primitive and homespun look with its deep dark saturated colors. Within a few years, Pam was sharing her love of this style by teaching others.

Since she began her teaching career, Pam has made over 100 quilts. She has been spreading her love of quilting through the teaching she has been doing since 2002. A number of her quilts have been featured in books published by C&T Publishing.

Instructions

1. Refer to Appliqué, pages 112 to 115, to make templates using Puppy pattern on page 61. Prepare appliqué pieces for 12 Puppy blocks.

2. Appliqué Puppies on 10" light background squares. (**Diagram 1**) Trim blocks to 9½" square.

Diagram 1

3. Place a 1¾" x 1¾" light square right sides together with a 1¾" x 9½" dark strip. Sew diagonally across square. (**Diagram 2**)

Diagram 2

Hint: *If you are unsure about sewing on a blank square, draw a diagonal line on wrong sides of 1¾" squares; sew along drawn line. (**Diagram 3**)*

Diagram 3

4. Trim about ¼" from stitching line. (**Diagram 4**)

Diagram 4

5. Flip resulting triangle over and press. (**Diagram 5**)

Diagram 5

6. Repeat steps 3 to 5 for opposite side of strip. (**Diagram 6**)

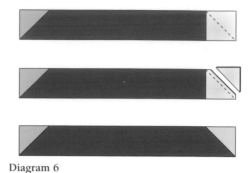

Diagram 6

7. Repeat steps 3 to 6 for remaining 1¾" x 9½" dark strips and 1¾" light squares.

8. Draw a diagonal line on wrong sides of 2⅛" light squares. (**Diagram 7**)

Diagram 7

9. Place two different 2⅛" light squares right sides together. Sew ¼" from each side of drawn line. (**Diagram 8**)

Diagram 8

10. Cut along drawn line to make two triangle squares. (**Diagram 9**) Press.

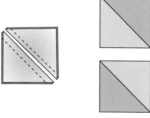

Diagram 9

11. Repeat steps 9 and 10 with remaining 2⅛" light squares.

12. Sew a pieced strip to opposite sides of appliqué block. (**Diagram 10**)

Diagram 10

13. Sew a triangle square from step 10 to opposite sides of a pieced strip; repeat. (**Diagram 11**)

Diagram 11

14. Sew strips to top and bottom of block. (**Diagram 12**)

Diagram 12

15. Repeat steps 12 to 14 for remaining appliqué blocks.
16. Place blocks together in four rows of three blocks. Sew blocks together in rows then sew rows together. (**Diagram 13**)

Diagram 13

17. Measure quilt top lengthwise. Cut two 1"-wide rust print strips to that length and sew to sides of quilt.
18. Measure quilt top crosswise. Cut two 1"-wide rust print strips to that length and sew to top and bottom of quilt.
19. Repeat steps 17 and 18 using 3"-wide dark brown strips.
20. Refer to Finishing Your Quilt, pages 121 to 127, to complete your quilt.

Puppy Love Quilt Layout

Puppy Appliqué

Made over 100 years ago, this quilt remains fresh today. Entered in quilt competitions in over seven state fairs, the quilt never failed to win a ribbon. Originally created by the painstaking and difficult method of piecing the arcs, the instructions have been modernized using the foundation piecing method which will enable today's quilter to make perfect rings with a minimum of stress.

Double Wedding Ring

by Florence McLaughlin Gray

Approximate Size
77½" x 77½"

Materials
6 yards white or off-white
½ yard each assorted solids (blue, green, pink, orange, yellow, gray, purple)
4½ yards backing
Batting
Copy paper (for paper foundations)

Patterns
Melon (Page 65)
Square (Page 66)
Arc Foundation A and B (page 67)
Ring Center (Page 68)
Quilting Patterns (pages 69 to 71)

Cutting
Note: *For the foundation-pieced arcs, you do not need to cut exact pieces. Read Foundation Piecing, pages 115 to 120, before beginning.*

40 Melons, white
16 Ring Centers, white
92 Squares, white
10 yards 2½"-wide bias strips, white (binding)

A real pioneer woman, Florence Gray satisfied her artistic love by making quilts. First in her home in Illinois, then while traveling by wagon train to settle on claims in the new Kansas territory.

When her two children were ready for advanced education, Florence became the matron of a dormitory at Southwestern Academy so that her children could complete their education.

When her daughter, who studied art, moved out of the dormitory, Florence complained that since her daughter was taking her pictures with her, Florence would take art lessons herself. She studied at the Academy for two years, becoming an accomplished watercolorist and oil painter.

She continued to make quilts incorporating her artistic talents in quilt designs. Her great-granddaughter, a professional artist, inherited Florence's oil paintings, her artistic proclivity and her quilts.

Instructions

1. Referring to Preparing the Foundation, make 80 Arc Foundations A and B. (**Diagram 1**)

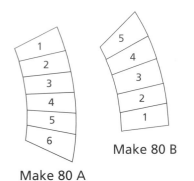

Make 80 A

Make 80 B

Diagram 1

2. Piece Arcs A and B. (**Diagram 2**)

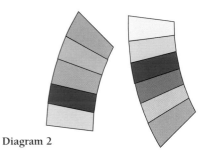

Diagram 2

3. Sew an Arc A to an Arc B at red lines. (**Diagram 3**) Repeat for remaining Arcs A and B.

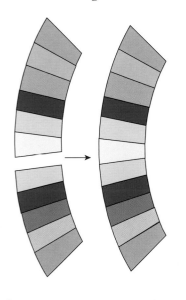

Diagram 3

4. Sew an Arc to a white Melon, matching midpoints. (**Diagram 4**)

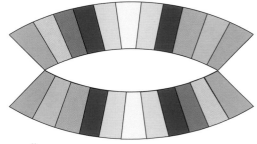

Diagram 4

5. Sew an Arc to other side of Melon. (**Diagram 5**)

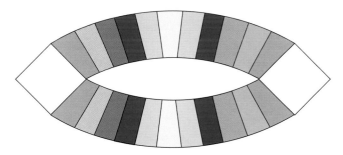

Diagram 5

6. Sew a white Square at each end of Arc/Melon unit. (**Diagram 6**)

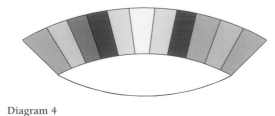

Diagram 6

Hint: *Sew Square to Arc from inner point to outer edge. Sew adjacent side in same manner.* (**Diagram 7**)

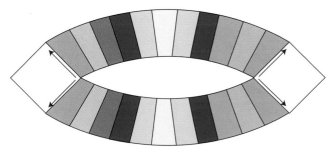

Diagram 7

7. Repeat steps 4 to 6 for remaining Arcs and Melons.

8. Lay out Arc/Melon units and Ring Centers in rows. Place white squares along all four sides. (**Diagram 8**)

Diagram 8

9. Sew Arc/Melon units to Ring Centers. Find midpoints of Melon and Arc; place right sides together, then use a pin to hold together at midpoint. Place a pin at each end. Sew with Ring Center on top.

10. Sew Arc/Melon units to top edges of Ring Centers.

11. Sew rows together.

12. Sew remaining Arc/Melon units to bottom edge.

13. Finish by insetting white squares along all four sides of the quilt top.

14. Refer to Finishing Your Quilt, pages 121 to 127, to complete your quilt. Referring to Quilt Layout on page 66, mark quilting designs from pages 69 to 71 onto quilt top.

Note: *Cut backing and batting even with quilt edge after quilting. Then attach bias binding along uneven edge.*

Melon Pattern

Double Wedding Ring Quilt Layout

Square Pattern

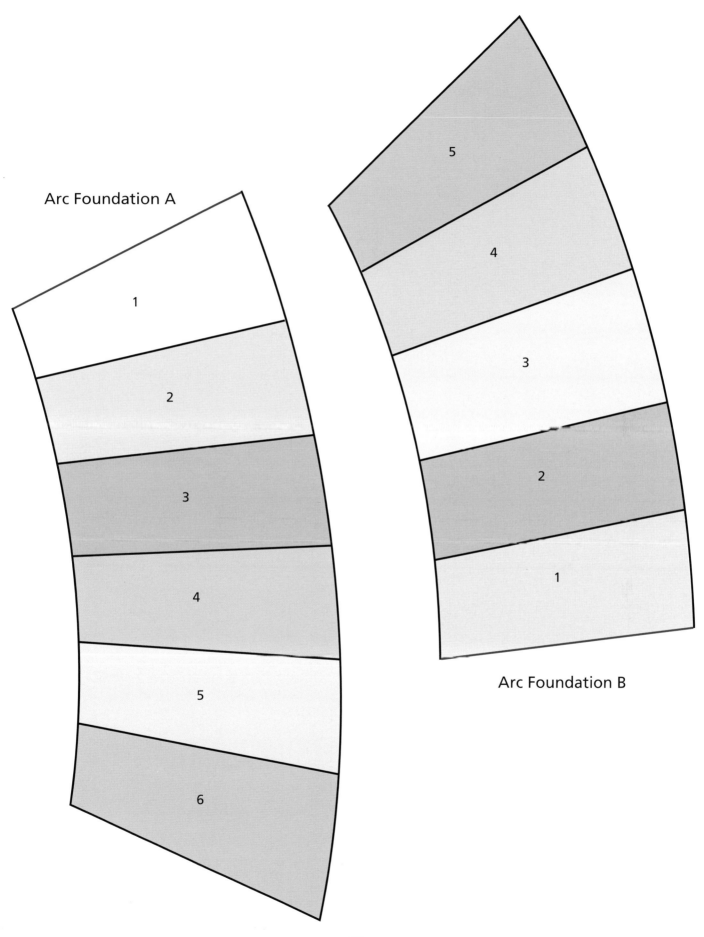

Arc Foundation A

Arc Foundation B

67

Ring Center (Quarter Pattern)

Pattern Note: *Trace Quarter Pattern onto template plastic. Rotate plastic a quarter turn and trace again. Rotate and trace twice more to create whole pattern.*

Bud
Quilting
Pattern

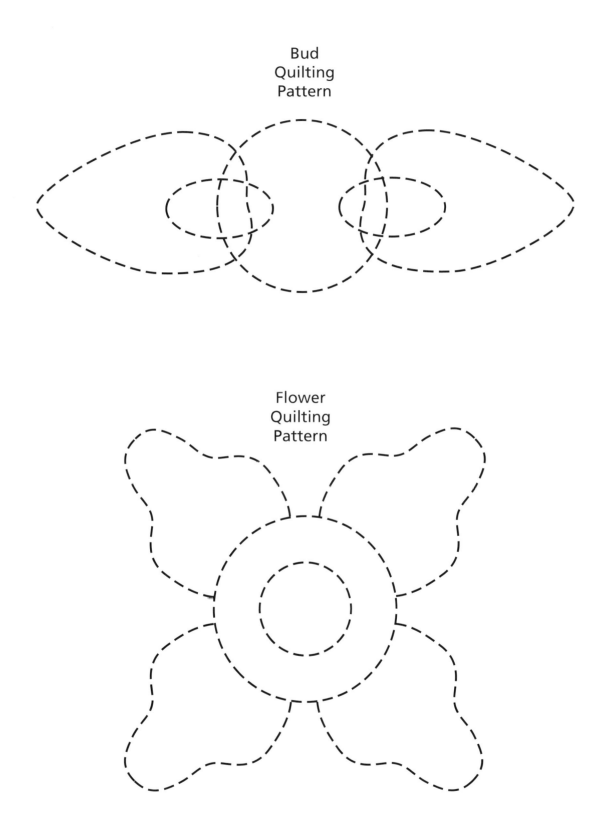

Flower
Quilting
Pattern

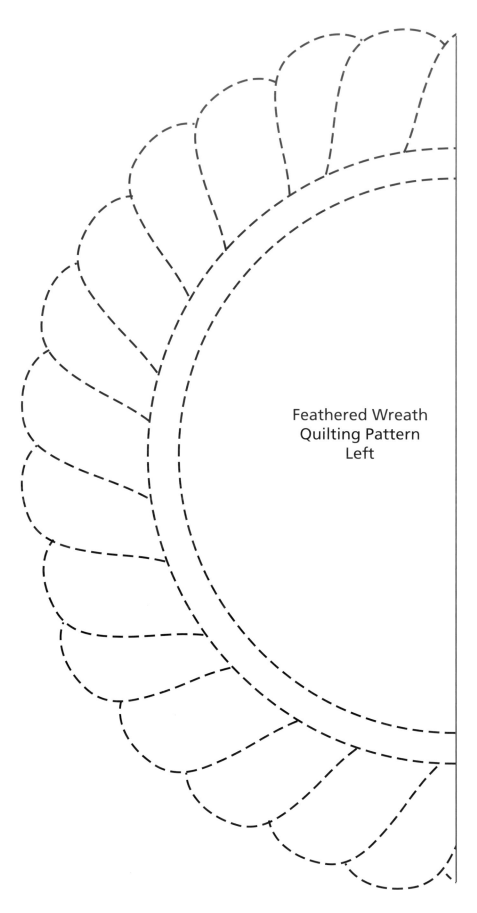

Feathered Wreath
Quilting Pattern
Left

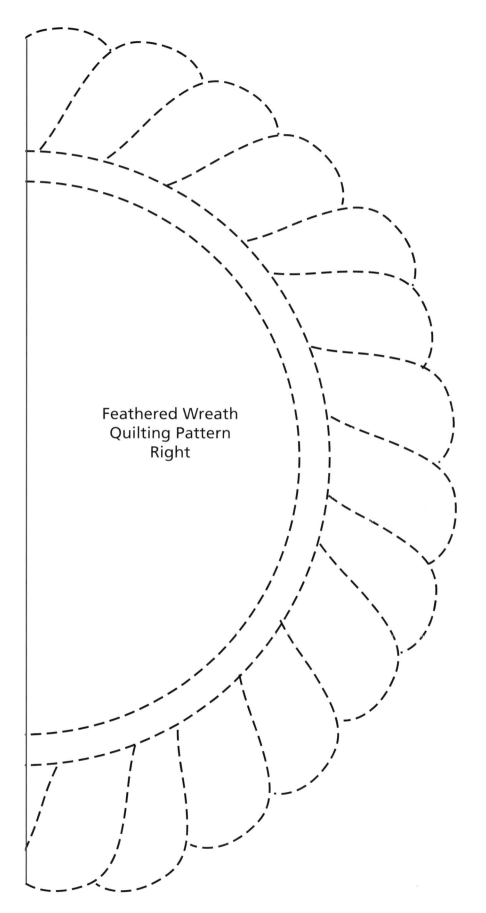

Feathered Wreath
Quilting Pattern
Right

Once the diamond background had been completed, the quilter decided it should become an undersea scene with fussy-cut motifs of beautiful tropical objects such as fish, turtles, seahorses, seaweed and shells. When the quilt had been quilted and embellished with yarns for seaweed and angelina fibers for light and sparkle, the quilter decided to take a deep breath, cut two 12" panels from each side and turned the entire quilt into a tryptich. The fantastic resulting quilt captured an award at the San Diego County Fair in 2006.

Ocean Paradise
by Betty Alofs

Approximate Size
48" x 20"

Materials
Assorted fat quarters of light, medium, and dark blues, greens, aquas, purples

Fat quarter each, medium and dark green (seaweed)

Undersea novelty prints (amount will depend on how many fish, sea shells, etc. that you can cut from the fabric)

Assorted fancy yarns, medium and dark green and matching thread (seaweed)

Iridescent Angelina® fiber

Iridescent yarn

Flannel (to use as a design board)

2 yards Lite Steam-a-Seam 2®

Batting

1½ yards backing

½ yard turquoise (binding)

Crystals (assorted sizes) and fabric glue

Patterns
Diamond (page 75)

Seaweed Top and Bottom (pages 76 and 77)

Jellyfish (page 77)

Cutting
300 assorted Diamonds, light, medium, and dark fat quarters

4 strips, 2½"-wide, turquoise (binding)

As a young girl, Betty Alofs sewed garments and home dec items. In1997, she took early retirement from her job as a technical editor and began to work in a friend's quilt shop. She was immediately smitten by the craft. She took classes, visited quilt shops and shows, attended teacher retreats and eventually began teaching at local shops.

She not only made quilts, but collected antique quilts as well. She enjoys trying to reproduce the look of antique quilts and embraces color and new techniques. Making quilts and teaching others what she has learned is a big part of her life now.

Betty has appeared on "America Quilts Creatively with Sue Hausmann" on PBS and "Simply Quilts with Alex Anderson" on HGTV. Her quilts have been accepted in many quilt shows, and this year she was honored as Artist in Residence at the Empty Spools Seminar in Pacific Grove, California.

Betty's other quilt "You've Got Mail" appears on page 104.

Instructions

1. Referring to photograph (page 72) and layout (page 75), arrange Diamonds so that there are light Diamonds in the center with the darkest Diamonds along the outside edges.
2. When you are pleased with your arrangement, sew the Diamonds together in rows. (**Diagram 1**)

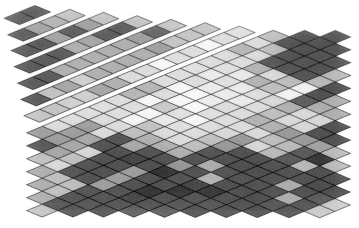

Diagram 1

3. Sew rows together. (**Diagram 2**)

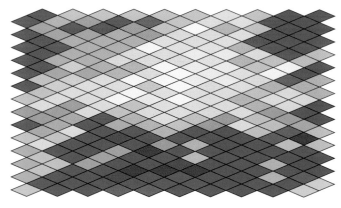

Diagram 2

4. Following manufacturer's directions, fuse Lite Steam-a-Seam 2® to wrong side of novelty prints.
5. Cut out individual fish, shells, and other sea creatures as desired.
6. Trace seaweed onto paper side of Lite Steam-a-Seam 2®. Fuse onto wrong side of medium and dark green fabrics. Cut out.

7. Cut medium and dark green yarns in assorted lengths. Couch to background using matching thread. Arrange fish, shells, sea creatures and seaweed as desired. Fuse in place. (**Diagram 3**)

Diagram 3

Hint: *Make a jellyfish using several layers of Angelina® fiber. Use pattern on page 77 to cut out shape. Sew to background along outside edges using machine zigzag and invisible thread. Couch 12" lengths of iridescent yarn strands along lower edge of jellyfish body.* (**Diagram 4**)

Diagram 4

Optional: *Sew a single layer of Angelina® fiber on top of light diamonds to add some sparkle.*

8. Trim all four sides of quilt ¼" from inner points. (**Diagram 5**)

Diagram 5

9. Refer to Finishing Your Quilt, pages 123 to 124, to layer and quilt your quilt.
10. Place quilted quilt onto cutting mat and cut into three separate sections.
11. Bind sections referring to Attaching the Continuous Machine Binding, pages 125 to 126.
12. For added sparkle, glue crystals on quilt using fabric glue.

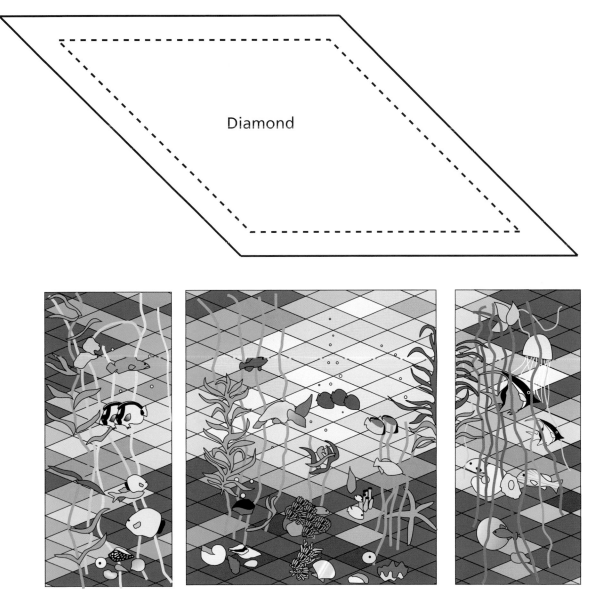

Diamond

Ocean Paradise Quilt Layout

Seaweed
(Top)

Seaweed
(Bottom)

Pattern Note: *When tracing Seaweed pattern, match red lines on top and bottom sections.*

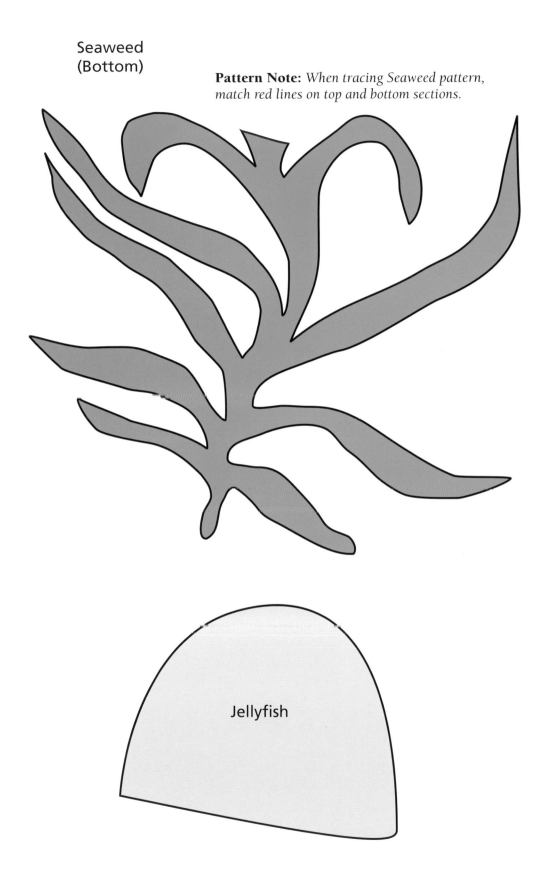

Jellyfish

Look closely at this prize-winning quilt, and it becomes apparent that it is a "Drunkard's Path" in a new guise. By combining luscious Japanese prints with beautiful machine-embroidered motifs, the quilt takes on an entirely new life and won the award for the Most Creative Design in the E. E. Schenck Company Trends Quilt Contest. The title is not actually a Japanese word. The quilter named it for her "adopted" son, Mike. "Mijo" is son in Spanish while the "chun" part of the name came from a character in a movie who walked like Mike. She wanted a name that would have meaning only to Mike and herself.

Mijochun

by Rosie Gonzalez

Approximate Size
49" x 70"

Materials
1/2 yard each of 10 assorted Japanese prints
3/4 yard light green solid
1 yard medium green solid (border, binding)
3 yards backing
Batting
Assorted machine embroidery threads
*Assorted Japanese motifs for machine embroidery
Template plastic

If you do not have a sewing machine that does embroidery, you can substitute fabric motifs. Fuse a lightweight paper-backed fusible web onto wrong side of fabric and cut out motifs. Remove paper backing and fuse in place on light green squares and rectangles. Use a machine zizag stitch and invisible nylon thread to tack down raw edges.

Patterns
Note: *When making templates, be sure to mark midpoint on each piece.*

Drunkard's Path A and B (page 83)

Cutting
Blocks
40 Drunkard's Path A, assorted Japanese prints
40 Drunkard's Path B, assorted Japanese prints
6 squares, 7 1/2" x 7 1/2", light green solid
4 rectangles, 7 1/2" x 14 1/2", light green solid

Finishing
6 strips, 1 1/2"-wide, medium green solid (first border)
Several strips, 1 1/2"-wide to 3"-wide, assorted Japanese prints (second border)
7 strips, 2 1/2"-wide, medium green solid (binding)

Rosie Gonzalez is the owner of a successful shop in San Diego that caters to quilters, crafters, sewers and embroiderers. She never intended, however, to be a quilter, much less a shop owner.

Twenty years ago, Rosie was making and selling fabric craft projects. She decided that if she could purchase fabric wholesale, she could resell what she didn't use to cover her expenses.

With $200 to spend, she and her husband drove to Los Angeles and purchased five bolts of fabric. They started selling fabric at yard sales and swap meets. Whenever they sold out, they returned to Los Angeles to buy more fabric.

When they could no longer carry the bolts of fabric in their truck, they decided to sell out of their garage. That went on for two years until they ran out of room and opened a storefront.

Rosie was still not a quilter, but she learned from her customers. She not only learned techniques, but she also became acquainted with what quilters wanted.

Today, 16 years later, Rosie has become a quilter, and her shop is the "home" to a lot of quilters.

Instructions

1. To make Drunkard's Path block, place A and B right sides together matching midpoints. Pin in place. (**Diagram 1**)

Hint: *Pick out A and P pieces randomly to give a more scrappy look.*

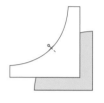

Diagram 1

2. Place a pin at each end. (**Diagram 2**)

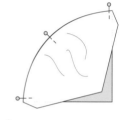

Diagram 2

3. Sew A and B along curve. (**Diagram 3**)

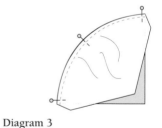

Diagram 3

4. Press seam toward B. (**Diagram 4**)

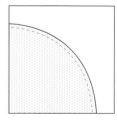

Diagram 4

5. Repeat steps for remaining Drunkard's Path blocks.

6. Machine embroider Japanese motifs on 7½" light green squares and 7½" x 14½" light green rectangles.

Note: *Use fabric motifs with paper-backed fusible web if you do not have machine embroidery capabilities on your sewing machine.*

7. Place Drunkard's Path blocks, embroidered squares and rectangles according to **Diagram 5**.

Diagram 5

8. Sew together in vertical rows; press seams. Sew rows together.

9. Measure quilt lengthwise. Cut two 1½"-wide medium green strips to that length. Sew to sides of quilt top.

10. Measure quilt crosswise. Cut two 1½"-wide medium green strips to that length. Sew to top and bottom of quilt.

11. For pieced border, sew assorted Japanese print strips together in sets of five. Press seams to one side. Cut strip sets at 3" intervals. (**Diagram 6**)

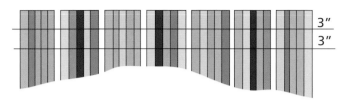

Diagram 6

12. Measure the quilt lengthwise. Sew the 3"-wide pieced strips together to make two strips to that measurement.

Note: *You may have to remove or trim strips to achieve the correct length.*

13. Sew pieced strips to sides of quilt. (**Diagram 7**)

Diagram 7

14. Measure the quilt crosswise. Sew 3"-wide pieced strips together to make two strips to that measurement. Sew pieced strips to top and bottom of quilt. (**Diagram 8**)

Diagram 8

15. Refer to Finishing Your Quilt, pages 121 to 127 to complete your quilt.

Mijochun Quilt Layout

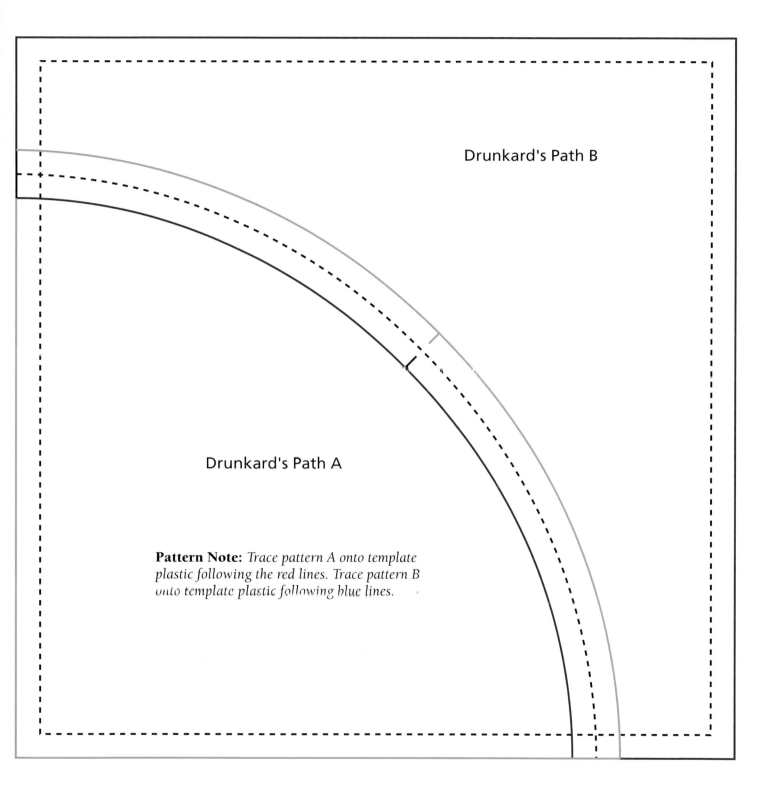

Drunkard's Path B

Drunkard's Path A

Pattern Note: *Trace pattern A onto template plastic following the red lines. Trace pattern B onto template plastic following blue lines.*

As the deadline for her quilt guild's "Wild, Wacky and Wonder-ful" challenge was approaching, the quilter began to panic. The challenge called for using three challenge fabrics: a bright sun-burst of colored lines on a yellow background, a blue and silver watery design and a dark purple with tiny darker purple flow-ers. She was stumped. Then she saw Tom Russell's delightful "Scrap Bag Bouquet" on the Scrap Bag Challenge episode of Home and Garden TV's Simply Quilts, and she knew what to do. The idea for the quilt came from that program; in fact the quilter feels that the "quilt is far more Tom Russell's than mine." The quilt placed first in the non-traditional quilts category and won the viewer's choice award.

Wild Flowers

by Lindy Sullivan

Approximate Size
35½" x 29½"

Materials
2½ yards black solid (background, border, backing)
Fat quarters of assorted blues, purples, oranges, greens (Circles)
Scraps red, yellow (smallest Circles)
³⁄₈ yard purple (binding)
Batting
2 yards paper-backed fusible web
Large red and black seed beads
Matching thread
Embroidery floss

Patterns
Large Flower Circle (page 90)
Large, Medium and Small Leaves (page 90)
Assorted Flower Circles (page 91)

Cutting
1 rectangle, 27½" x 20½", black
several strips, ³⁄₄" to 2" wide, assorted fat quarters (Circles)
2 strips, ³⁄₄" x 4½", black (first border - sides)
2 strips, ³⁄₄" x 17", multi-colored print (first border - sides)
2 strips, ³⁄₄" x 18½", multi-colored print (first border - top and bottom)
2 strips, ³⁄₄" x 4", black (first border - top and bottom)
2 strips, ³⁄₄" x 14", black (first border - top and bot-tom)
2 strips, 4" x 20½", black (second border)
2 strips, 4" x 35½", black (second border)
4 strips, 2½"-wide, purple (binding)

Lindy Sullivan never intended to make a quilt when she stepped into her first quilt shop. She was interested in making sculpted dolls, and the shop offered classes in dollmaking.

She loved starting with scraps of fabric and ending up with something three dimensional and silly—something that could make her laugh.

Wanting to expand her skills and meet other dollmakers, she was advised to join a quilt guild. The guild, however, didn't yield any fellow dollmakers; instead, Lindy ended up falling in love with quilts and never went back to dollmaking.

Today, Lindy lives with a sweetheart and a cat, both of whom she says are dangerous companions for a quilter: the sweetheart because his response to her purchasing of fabric is in-variably, "Does fabric go bad?" and the cat because he adores quilts and is only happy if he is sit-ting squarely in the middle of one.

Instructions

1. Sew assorted orange strips together to make a square about 12" x 12". (**Diagram 1**) Repeat for another pieced square using blues and purples. Press seams open. (**Diagram 2**)

Diagram 1

Diagram 2

Note: *Make as many pieced fabric squares as needed for your quilt.*

2. Trace assorted sizes of Circles onto the paper side of fusible web. Following manufacturer's directions, iron fusible web Circles to wrong side of pieced fabric squares. (**Diagram 3**)

Note: *Fuse smallest Cirles to wrong side of red and orange fabrics.*

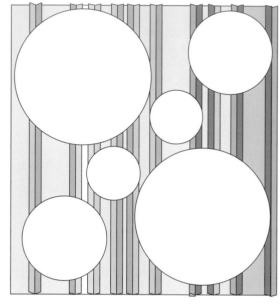

Diagram 3

3. Cut out circles along drawn lines.

4. Sew two green strips together; press seams open. Draw nine Large Leaves, six Medium Leaves and two Small Leaves onto paper side of fusible web. Rough cut leaves. Place Leaves with center tips lined up along seam of sewn green strips. (**Diagram 4**) Fuse Leaves in place and cut out along drawn lines.

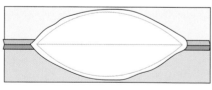

Diagram 4

5. Remove paper from Circles and Leaves; set aside.

6. For the borders, sew a $3/4$" x $4^{1}/2$" black strip to a $3/4$" x 17" multi-colored strip. Sew strip to 4" x $20^{1}/2$" black strip. (**Diagram 5**) Repeat.

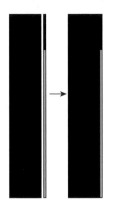

Diagram 5

7. Sew strips to opposite sides of $27^{1}/2$" x $20^{1}/2$" black rectangle. (**Diagram 6**)

Diagram 6

8. Sew $3/4$" x 4" black strip to $3/4$" x $18^{1}/2$" multi-colored strip; sew a $3/4$" x 14" black strip to other end of multi-colored strip; sew strip to 4" x $35^{1}/2$" black strip. (**Diagram 7**) Repeat.

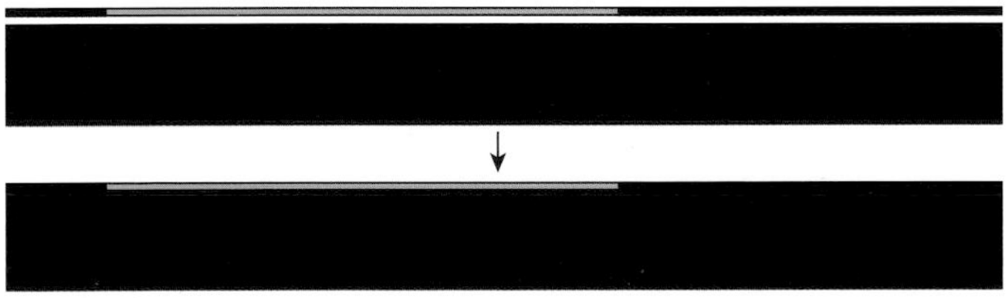

Diagram 7

9. Sew strips to top and bottom of black rectangle.

10. Place the black rectangle with right side up on a flat ironing surface. Arrange Circles and Leaves referring to Layout and photograph for placement or make your own design. Iron the Circles and Leaves in place referring to manufacturer's directions for fusible web.

11. Topstitch, then blanket stitch by machine around edges of Circles and Leaves. Sew beads around edges of Circles and down center of Leaves. (**Diagram 8**)

Diagram 8

Note: *If your sewing machine does not do a blanket stitch, you can stitch by hand. (**Diagram 9**)*

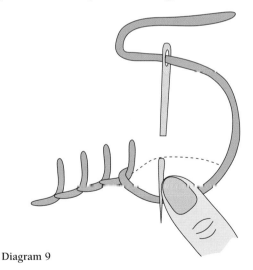

Diagram 9

12. Refer to Finishing Your Quilt, pages 121 to 127, to complete your quilt.

Wild Flowers Quilt Layout

Lindy had so much fun designing her quilt top that she decided to make another quilt for the back!

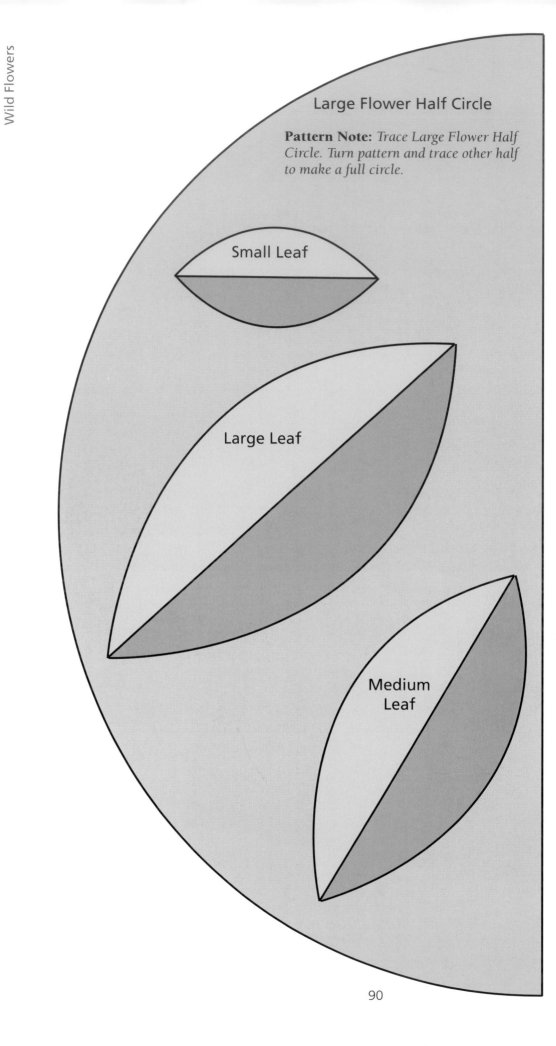

Large Flower Half Circle

Pattern Note: *Trace Large Flower Half Circle. Turn pattern and trace other half to make a full circle.*

Small Leaf

Large Leaf

Medium Leaf

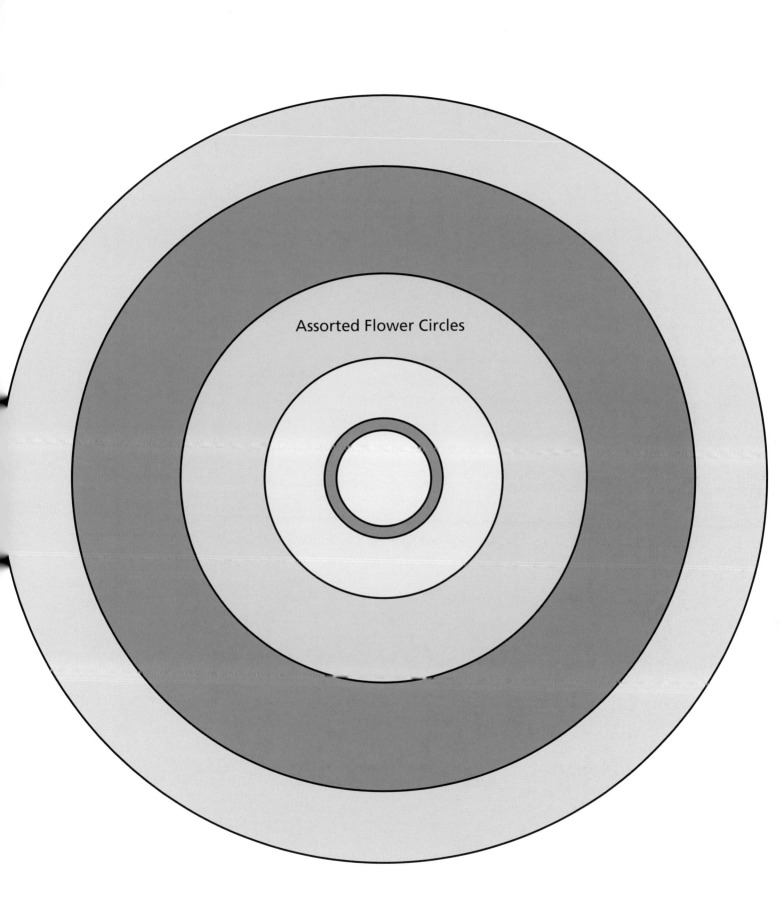

Assorted Flower Circles

The old fabrics in this quilt are evidence that this quilt was probably made early in the last century. There is a great deal of variation in the work in the different squares in this quilt, an indication that the squares were not made by one person. Instead, the quilt could have been made by various members of a social group and eventually presented to the owner. Nevertheless, the quilt owner entered this quilt in a number of state fairs and always won a ribbon. While foundation piecing has experienced a resurgence in the past few years, this quilt is evidence that foundation piecing of some patterns was popular over 100 years ago.

Pineapple Log Cabin

by Clara Gail Wilson

Approximate Size
64" x 77"

Materials
Assorted dark scraps and fat quarters totalling 6 yards
Assorted light scraps and fat quarters totalling $3^1/4$ yards
$1^1/4$ yards pink solid (first border and binding)
$1^1/4$ yards muslin (second border)
4 yards backing
Batting

Pattern
Pineapple Log Cabin - quarter pattern (page 96)

Cutting
Note: *Cut light and dark fabrics into strips $^1/2$" wider than the spaces they are to cover.*

20 squares, $2^1/2$" x $2^1/2$", pink/red (centers)
40 squares, 4" x 4", dark (cut in half diagonally for corners, space 17)
7 strips, $2^1/2$"-wide, pink solid (first border)
8 strips, $4^1/2$"-wide, muslin (second border)
8 strips, $2^1/2$"-wide, pink solid (binding)

The youngest of eight children, Clara Gail Wilson was born in Illinois in 1908. For the first part of her adult life, she was the caregiver for her sick mother as well as the housekeeper for the family.

After her mother's death, Clara returned to school receiving a degree, which allowed her to teach for the next twenty years until she retired.

There is no evidence that Clara actually made this quilt although she came from a family of quilters. She was active in many local church and education associations, women's groups and social clubs. The quilt was obviously made by several quilters, and it is possible that Clara was presented with this quilt by the members of one of these groups.

Instructions

1. Make 20 foundations referring to Preparing the Foundation, page 115.

Note: *You will need to copy four patterns from page 96 and tape together to make each foundation.* (**Diagram 1**)

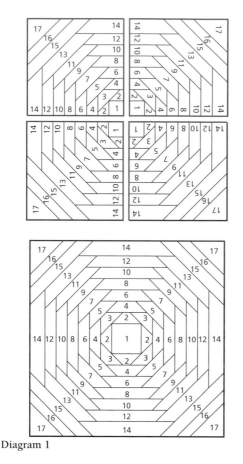

Diagram 1

2. Make 20 Pineapple Log Cabin blocks referring to Making the Block, pages 116 to 118. Use light and dark fabrics referring to positions of light and dark. (**Diagram 2**)

Diagram 2

3. Place blocks in five rows of four. Sew blocks together in rows then sew rows together. (**Diagram 3**)

Diagram 3

4. Measure quilt lengthwise. Piece and cut two $2^1/2$"-wide pink strips to that length. Sew to sides of quilt. Measure quilt crosswise. Piece and cut two $2^1/2$"-wide pink strips to that length. Sew to top and bottom of quilt.

5. Repeat step 4 for second border using $4^1/2$"-wide muslin strips.

6. Refer to Finishing your Quilt, pages 121 to 127, to complete your quilt.

Pineapple Log Cabin Quilt Layout

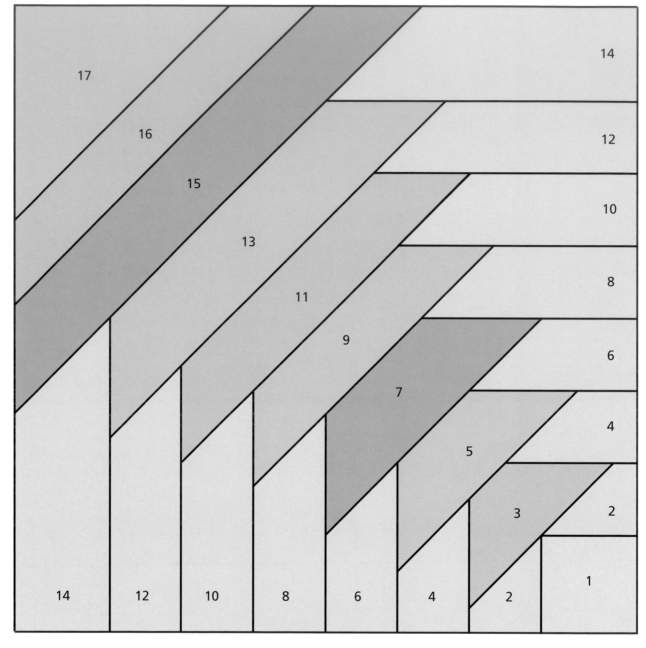

Quarter Pineapple Log Cabin
Foundation

Inspired by a design on a picture postcard and without a pattern, the quilter created this quilt, making it up as she went. All of the flowers are made of yoyos while the leaves are just folded circles with raw edges. The flowers and leaves are all made by hand and placed over the machine-pieced background. The quilt received a ribbon at the Orange County Fair in 2001.

Cottage Door

by Ada LeClaire

Approximate Size
26" x 30"

Materials
Assorted fat quarters dark florals, medium florals, medium greens, light rusts, light florals, dark rusts, white, beige, brown (cottage door)

Assorted scraps yellow, orange, purple, and green (flowers and leaves)

$3/4$ yard brown print (border)

1 yard backing fabric

$1/2$ yard black (binding)

Batting

5 yards $1/4$"-wide purchased fusible bias tape, black matching thread

Optional: *1 yard fusible interfacing grid*

Patterns
$1^1/2$", 2", $2^1/2$", and 3" Circles (page 102)

Cutting
Cottage Door

17 squares, $1^3/4$" x $1^3/4$", dark florals

18 squares, $1^3/4$" x $1^3/4$", medium florals

60 squares, $1^3/4$" x $1^3/4$", medium greens

8 squares, $1^3/4$" x $1^3/4$", light rusts

8 squares, $1^3/4$" x $1^3/4$", light florals

33 squares, $1^3/4$" x $1^3/4$", dark rusts

16 squares, $1^3/4$" x $1^3/4$", white

24 squares, $1^3/4$" x $1^3/4$", brown

8 squares, $1^3/4$" x $1^3/4$", beige

Flowers and Leaves

50 - $2^1/2$" Circles, yellow

17 - $2^1/2$" Circles, orange

25 - $1^1/2$" Circles, orange

16 - 3" Circles, orange

21 - 2" Circles, purple

81 - $1^1/2$" Circles, green

Ada LeClair began quilting by doing all of her piecing and quilting by hand. Eventually she was forced to switch to machine piecing because she felt that there were too many patterns to make and not enough time for all that hand piecing.

Eventually even hand quilting had become too time consuming, and Ada became a long arm machine quilter. Her love of hand quilting, however, continues, and she tries to make at least one hand-quilted project each year.

Ada's "Asian Influence" quilt appears on page 10.

Finishing

2 strips, 6" x 20½", brown print (border)
2 strips, 6" x 26½", brown print (border)
4 strips, 2½"-wide, black (binding)

Instructions

1. Lay out 1¾" squares in rows according to **Diagram 1**.

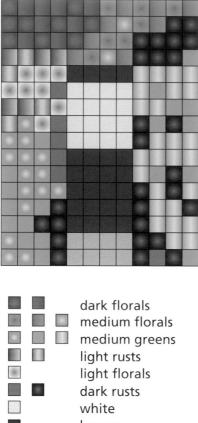

dark florals
medium florals
medium greens
light rusts
light florals
dark rusts
white
brown
beige

Diagram 1

2. Sew squares in rows. Press seams for rows in alternating directions. (**Diagram 2**) Sew rows together.

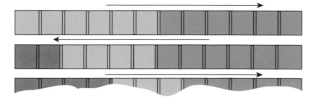

Diagram 2

Optional: *Use interfacing grid to make sewing small squares easier. Place interfacing bumpy side up on a flat ironing surface. Position squares with edges butting up against each other on interfacing using grid as a guide. Fuse squares in place following manufacturer's directions. Fold first vertical row right sides together with second row; sew using a ?" seam allowance. (**Diagram 3**)*

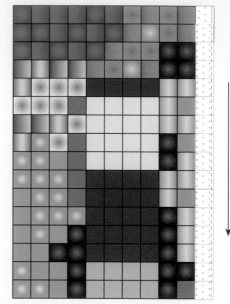

Diagram 3

*Continue sewing in same manner until all vertical rows are sewn. (**Diagram 4**)*

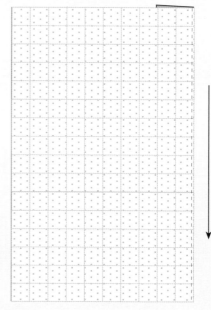

Diagram 4

Snip seams where horizontal rows meet and press seams for adjacent rows in opposite directions. (**Diagram 5**)

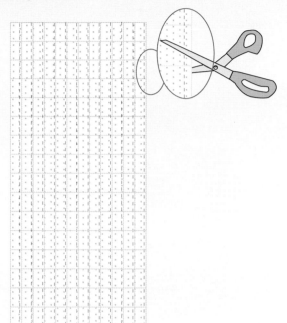

Diagram 5

Sew horizontal rows together to finish cottage door. (**Diagram 6**)

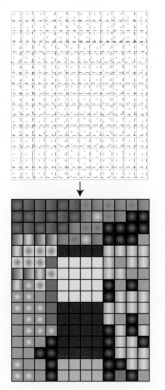

Diagram 6

3. Cut 11 pieces of $^1/4$"-wide black fusible bias tape, 5" long. Referring to **Diagram 7**, fuse eight pieces horizontally on door and three pieces vertically on door window. Cut two 15" pieces of fusible bias tape and fuse vertically along each side of door. Sew bias tape in place using a wide zigzag stitch and black thread or a row of straight stitching along each side of each strip.

Diagram 7

4. For border, sew a 6" x $20^1/2$" brown print strip to each side of quilt top. Sew a 6" x $26^1/2$" brown print strip to top and bottom. Cut and fuse $^1/4$" wide black bias tape over seams between cottage door and border. (**Diagram 8**)

Diagram 8

5. Refer to Finishing Your Quilt, pages 121 to 127, to layer and quilt.

6. Make yoyos using the yellow, orange and purple Circles. Fold the edge of each circle about 1/4" toward wrong side. (**Diagram 9**)

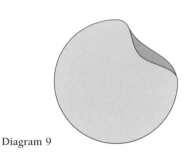

Diagram 9

7. Using a needle and thread, sew a running stitch near fold. (**Diagram 10**)

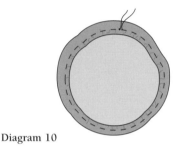

Diagram 10

8. Pull thread and tie knot. (**Diagram 11**)

Diagram 11

9. Flatten resulting yoyo so hole is in center. (**Diagram 12**)

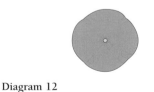

Diagram 12

10. Referring to photograph and quilt layout, tack centers of yoyos to cottage door.

11. To make leaves, fold green Circle in half with wrong sides together. Using a needle and thread, sew running stitches across one end of folded Circle. (**Diagram 13**)

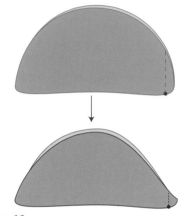

Diagram 13

12. Pull stitches until tight and tie knot. Repeat for all green Circles.

13. Referring to photograph and quilt layout, tuck leaves under yoyo flowers and tack in place with a few stitches. Leaves ends loose.

14. Refer to Adding the Continuous Machine Binding and Adding a Rod Pocket, pages 125 to 127, to finish your quilt.

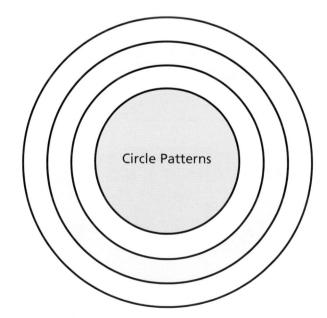

Circle Patterns

Cottage Door Quilt Layout

Along Hope Street, a country dirt road in Ramona, California, stand 30 to 40 mailboxes in a row. The sight inspired the quilter to create this quilt. The local San Diego County Fair seemed a good place to display this quilt since many people in the area would be familiar with Hope Street's mailboxes. The quilt captured a second place ribbon in the 2006 competition.

You've Got Mail

by Betty Alofs

Approximate Size
20½" x 18"

Materials
Scraps green, brown, gray, red (mailboxes)
¼ yard blue (sky)
⅜ yard green (grass)
⅜ yard brown (road)
⅝ yard backing
¼ yard red (binding, lettering)
Batting
Black fabric pen
1 yard Lite Steam-a-Seam 2®
Green, gold, gray embroidery floss
Green sewing thread
White typewriter correction fluid or fabric paint

Patterns
Mailboxes and Rocks (pages 109 and 110)
Trees (page 111)
Street Sign (page 111)

Cutting
13" x 29" rectangles, green, brown
8" x 28½" rectangle, blue
2½"-wide strips, red (binding)

Betty Alofs had been sewing for many years when she discovered quilting and fell in love with it right away.

Her main focus now is creating pictorial patterns for realistic appliquéd quilts and wall hangings from photos. The excitement builds from the application of the right color, value, texture and perspective. When it is just right, she has a feeling of satisfaction knowing that she has reached her goal of transforming sometimes difficult scenes into beautiful appliquéd pieces.

Part of the satisfaction is the discovery of just the perfect fabric for her pieces and using thread and embellishments to bring the piece to life.

Betty has recently revealed her secrets in her first book just recently published, *Quilt Your Favorite Photos*. She considers that book to be her greatest achievement.

Betty's "Ocean Paradise" appears on page 72.

Instructions

1. Read Fusible Appliqué, page 114 to 115, and pre-pare Mailboxes, Trees, Street Sign, and Rocks for fusible appliqué.

Note: *For the words "You've Got Mail!," hand draw on tracing paper first, then trace onto paper side of paper-backed fusible web.*

2. Cut triangular shapes for road and grass referring to **Diagram 1**.

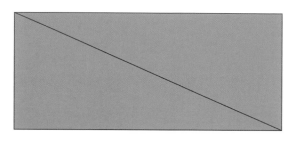

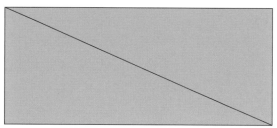

Diagram 1

3. Sew the pieces together along the diagonal edge. (**Diagram 2**) Press seams open.

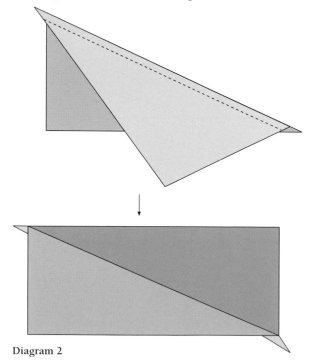

Diagram 2

4. Sew road/grass to sky fabric. (**Diagram 3**) Press seam open. **Note:** *The sky and road/grass pieces do not have to line up exactly. The edges will be trimmed later.*

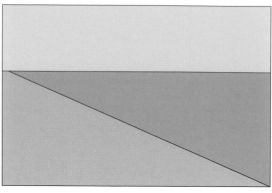

Diagram 3

5. Trim backing so it measures $21^{1}/_{2}$" x 19". (**Diagram 4**)

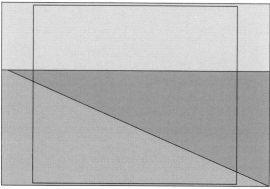

Diagram 4

6. Place mailboxes and rocks along right edge of road. (**Diagram 5**) Remove paper backing and referring to manufacturer's directions, iron to fuse in place.

Diagram 5

7. Place trees (in numerical order starting at the left edge) along top edge of grass, removing paper backing from Trees as you go; remover paper and position Street Sign along right edge of grass. When sign and trees are in place, carefully press to fuse. (**Diagram 6**)

Diagram 6

8. Remove paper backing and arrange lettering "You've Got Mail" across the sky and fuse in place. (**Diagram 7**)

Diagram 7

9. Use a machine satin stitch and matching thread, stitch around mailboxes adding detail on front of mailboxes. (**Diagram 8**)

Diagram 8

10. Using a machine blanket stitch and green thread, sew along top edge of grass and top edge of road under mailboxes. (**Diagram 9**)

Diagram 9

Note: *If your sewing machine does not have a blanket stitch, use a hand Blanket stitch.* (***Diagram 10***)

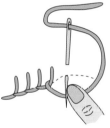

Diagram 10

11. Using Backstitch and two to three strands of gray, green and gold embroidery floss, stitch "grassy" details along lower edges of mailboxes. (**Diagram 11**)

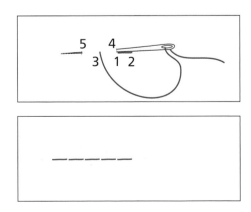

Diagram 11

12. Make mailbox shadows using a black fabric pen with a light touch. Use the side edge of the pen.
13. Referring to photo, make simple latches on mailbox fronts using the black fabric pen.
14. Using white typewriter correction fluid, write street name on sign.

Hint: *Use your own street name for a personal touch. Make the green rectangle large enough to fit your street name.*

15. Refer to Finishing Your Quilt, pages 121 to 127, to complete your quilt.

You've Got Mail Quilt Layout

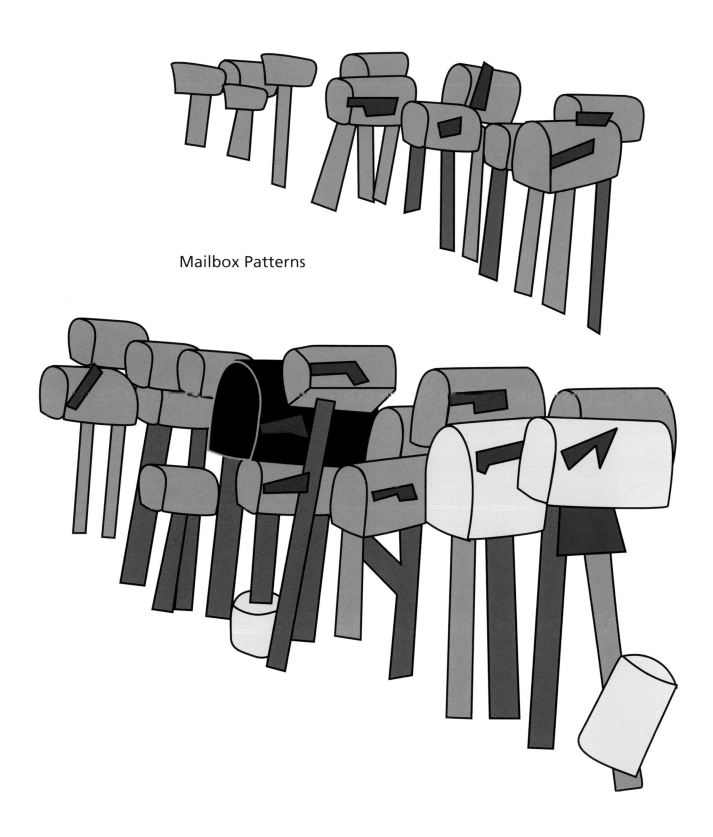

Mailbox Patterns

Mailbox and Rock Patterns

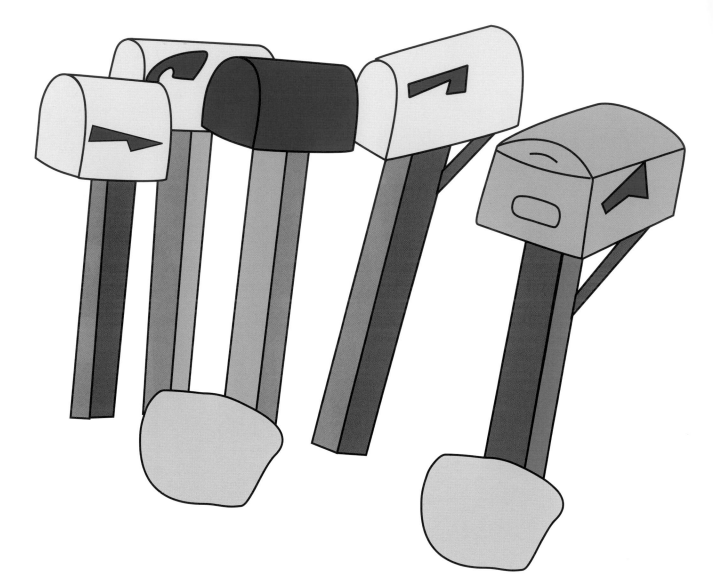

Tree Patterns

Street Sign Pattern

General Directions

Before You Begin—A Word About Fabric

For over a hundred years, quilts have been made with 100% cotton fabric, and this remains today the fabric of choice for most quilters.

There are many properties in cotton that make it especially well suited to quiltmaking. There is less distortion in cotton fabric, thereby affording the quilter greater security in making certain that even the smallest bits of fabric will fit together. Because a quilt block made of cotton can be ironed flat with a steam iron, a puckered area, created by mistake, can be fixed. The sewing machine needle can move through cotton with a great deal of ease when compared to some synthetic fabrics. While you may find that quilt artists today often use other kinds of fabric to create the quilts quickly and accurately, 100% cotton is strongly recommended.

Cotton fabric today is produced in so many wonderful and exciting combinations of prints and solids that it is often difficult to pick colors for your quilt. We've chosen our favorite colors for these quilts, but don't be afraid to make your own choices

For years, quilters were advised to prewash all of their fabric to test for colorfastness and shrinkage. Now most quilters don't bother to prewash all of their fabric but they do pretest. Cut a strip about 2" wide from each piece of fabric that you will use in your quilt. Measure both the length and the width of the strip. Then immerse it in a bowl of very hot water, using a separate bowl for each piece of fabric. Be especially concerned about reds and dark blues because they have a tendency to bleed if the initial dyeing was not done properly. If it's one of your favorite fabrics that's bleeding, you might be able to salvage the fabric. Try washing the fabric in very hot water until you've washed out all of the excess dye. Unfortunately, fabrics that continue to bleed after they have been washed repeatedly will bleed forever. So eliminate them right at the start.

Now, take each one of the strips and iron them dry with a hot iron. Be especially careful not to stretch the strip. When the strips are completely dry, measure and compare them to the size of your original strip. If all of your fabric is shrinking the same amount, you don't have to worry about uneven shrinkage in your quilt. When you wash the final quilt, the puckering that will result may give you the look of an antique quilt. If you don't want this look, you are going to have to wash and dry all of your fabric before you start cutting. Iron the fabric using some spray starch or sizing to give the fabric a crisp finish.

If you are never planning to wash your quilt, i.e. your quilt is intended to be a wall hanging, you could eliminate the pre-testing process. You may run the risk, however, of some future relative to whom you have willed your quilts deciding that the wall hanging needs freshening by washing.

Before beginning to work, make sure that your fabric is absolutely square. If it is not, you will have difficulty cutting square pieces. Fabric is woven with crosswise and lengthwise threads. Lengthwise threads should be parallel to the selvage (that's the finished edge along the sides; sometimes the fabric company prints its name along the selvage), and crosswise threads should be perpendicular to the selvage. If fabric is off grain, you can usually straighten it by pulling gently on the true bias in the opposite direction to the off-grain edge. Continue doing this until the crosswise threads are at a right angle to the lengthwise threads.

Appliqué

Hand Appliqué

Supplies

For hand appliqué there are a few basic supplies that you will need—many of which will most likely be found in your sewing basket.

Needles: Use a needle that is comfortable for you to work with. It can be a *sharp*—general use needle, a *between*—used mainly for hand quilting or even a *straw* needle—extra fine sewing needle. As long as it is sharp and easy for you to handle, it will work for appliqué.

Thread: Use 100 percent cotton thread that matches the color of the piece you are appliquéing. A thin-weight thread such as #60 is recommended.

Pins: Use thin, sharp pins that are short in length to help keep your thread from getting tangled.

Freezer paper: Use freezer paper—found in most grocery stores—for the templates for your appliqué.

Thimble: Use a well-fitted thimble when you appliqué.

Iron: Use an iron to press seam allowances onto freezer paper. The small craft irons available today are wonderful to use.

Technique

Trace pattern pieces onto the dull side of freezer paper. Be sure to trace each piece the number of times that pattern will be used in your project. (**Diagram 1**) Cut freezer paper along drawn lines.

Diagram 1

Place freezer paper pattern shiny side up onto wrong side of fabric; pin in place. Cut out fabric about ¼" from the edge of the freezer paper. (**Diagram 2**)

Diagram 2

Clip seam allowances along inside curves. Never clip outside curves. (**Diagram 3**)

Diagram 3

Using a hot iron, press seam allowance onto freezer paper. The heat of the iron will cause the shiny side of freezer paper to adhere temporarily to the fabric. (**Diagram 4**)

Diagram 4

Prepare all appliqué pieces in the same manner. Do not remove freezer paper. Cut background fabric the size specified in the project directions; press. For placement guides, fold background in half, then in quarters. (**Diagram 5**)

Diagram 5

Place background on a flat ironing surface. Using the photograph and/or placement guide, position the first piece on background fabric. Continue placing appliqué pieces until a pleasing arrangement is achieved. (**Diagram 6**)

Diagram 6

Iron pieces in place, then baste or pin. Note: Ironing pieces will only provide a temporary hold, therefore pinning or basting is necessary.

Stitch edges of appliqués using matching thread and an invisible stitch. (**Diagram 7**)

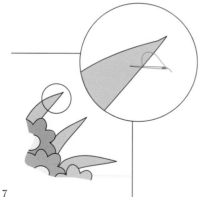

Diagram 7

When all pieces are appliquéd in place, carefully make slits in the background fabric and remove freezer paper. Cut away fabric about $1/4$" from stitching lines. (**Diagram 8**)

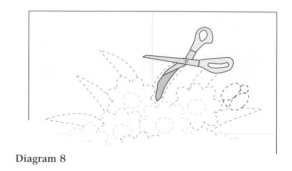

Diagram 8

Two-Layer Designs

Some appliqué pieces such as the flowers in *Wild Flowers*, page 84, are made up of two layers. It is best to appliqué the top layer onto the bottom first before appliquéing to background fabric. Place the top (center) piece onto the Petal piece and appliqué in place. Turn Petal piece over, make a small slit and remove freezer paper and trim backing $1/4$" from stitching. (**Diagram 9**)

Diagram 9

Fusible Appliqué

There are many different paper-backed fusible products on the market today. Each has its own unique characteristics that will help you decide which to use when making a quilt. Always be sure to follow the manufacturer's directions as each product differs greatly.

You've Got Mail, page 104, uses a lightweight paper-backed fusible web such as Lite Steam-a-Seam 2® by The Warm™ Company. This will enable you to use a machine zigzag to appliqué the edges. Using a heavyweight brand will cause your needle to gum up and possibly break.

Trace the patterns onto the paper side of the fusible web following the manufacturer's directions. Be especially careful because pattern pieces that are not symmetrical will end up as mirror images of the finished project. Cut out the pattern pieces from the fusible web.

Now position fusible web pattern with paper side up onto wrong side of fabric; fuse in place with hot iron. **Note:** *Refer to manufacturer's directions for heating setting and pressing time for the product you are using.*

Machine Appliqué

Using a machine Zigzag or Blanket stitch and matching or invisible thread, stitch along all raw edges of appliqué. You may want to practice on another piece of fabric to see which zigzag width and length works best for you.

Foundation Piecing

Materials

Before you begin, decide the kind of foundation on which you are planning to piece the blocks.

Paper

The most popular choice for foundation piecing is paper. It's readily available and fairly inexpensive. You can use copy paper, newsprint, tracing paper—even computer paper. The paper does not remain a permanent part of your quilt as it is removed once the blocks are completely sewn.

Fabric

If you choose to hand piece your block, you may want to choose fabric as your foundation. Just remember that fabric is not removed after you make your block so you will have another layer to quilt through. This may be a problem if you are planning to hand quilt. Using fabric might be an advantage, however, if you want to use some non-traditional quilting fabrics, such as satin, since the fabric foundation will add stability to the block. Fabric makes a good choice for crazy quilts. If you do decide to use fabric, choose a lightweight and light-colored fabric, such as muslin, that will allow you to see through for ease in tracing.

Other Materials

Another option for foundation materials is Tear Away™ or Fun-dation™, translucent non-woven materials combining both the advantages of both paper and fabric. They are easy to see through, but like paper they can be removed with ease.

Currently a new kind of foundation material has appeared in the market place: a foundation paper that dissolves in water after use. Two companies, W.H. Collins and EZ Quilting by Wrights are producing this product.

Preparing the Foundation

Place your foundation material over your chosen block and trace the block pattern. Use a ruler and a fine-line pencil or permanent marker, and make sure that all lines are straight. Sometimes short dashed lines or even dotted lines are easier to make. Be sure to copy all numbers. You will need to make a foundation for each block you are planning to use.

If you have a home copier, you can copy your tracing on the copy machine. Since the copy machine might slightly alter the measurements of the block, make certain that you copy each block from the original pattern.

You can also scan the block if you have a home scanner and then print out the required number of blocks.

Cutting the Fabric

In foundation piecing, you do not have to cut perfect shapes!

You can, therefore, use odd pieces of fabric: squares, strips, and rectangles. The one thing you must remember, however, is that every piece must be at least $1/4$" larger on all sides than the space it is going to cover. Strips and squares are easy: just measure the length and width of the needed space and add $1/2$" all around. Cut your strip to that measurement. Triangles, however, can be a bit tricky. In that case, measure the widest point of the triangle and cut your fabric about $1/2$" to 1" wider.

Other Supplies for Foundation Piecing

Piecing by Hand

You will need a reasonably thin needle such as a Sharp size 10, a good quality neutral-colored thread such as size 50 cotton, some pins, a glue stick, fabric scissors, muslin or fabric for the bases.

Piecing by Machine

You will need a cleaned and oiled sewing machine, glue stick, pins, paper scissors, fabric scissors, foundation material.

Before beginning to sew your actual block by machine, determine the proper stitch length. Use a piece of the paper you are planning to use for the foundation and draw a straight line on it. Set your machine so that it sews with a fairly short stitch (about 20 stitches per inch). Sew along the line. If you can tear the paper apart with ease, you are sewing with the right length. You don't want to sew with such a short stitch that the paper falls apart by itself. If you are going to use a fabric foundation with the sewing machine, use the stitch length you normally use.

Using a Pattern

The numbers on the block show the order in which the pieces are to be placed and sewn on the base. It is extremely important that you follow the numbers; otherwise the entire process won't work.

Making the Block

The important thing to remember about making a foundation block is that the fabric pieces go on the unmarked side of the foundation while you sew on the printed side. The finished blocks are a mirror image of the original pattern.

Hold the foundation up to a light source—even a window pane—with the unmarked side facing. Find the space marked 1 on the unmarked side and put a dab of glue there.

Place the fabric right side up on the unmarked side on Space 1, making certain that the fabric overlaps at least 1/4" on all sides of space 1. (**Diagram 10**)

Diagram 10

With right sides together, place Fabric Piece 2 on Fabric Piece 1, making sure that the edge of Piece 2 is even with the edge of Piece 1. (**Diagram 11**)

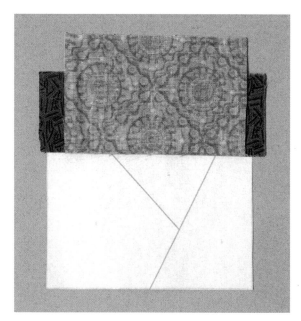

Diagram 11

116

To make certain that Piece 2 will cover Space 2, fold the fabric piece back along the line between Space 1 and Space 2. (**Diagram 12**)

Diagram 12

With the marked side of the foundation facing up, place the piece on the sewing machine (or sew by hand), holding both Piece 1 and Piece 2 in place. Sew along the line between Space 1 and Space 2. (**Diagram 13**)

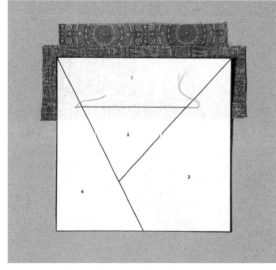

Diagram 13

Hint: *If you use a small stitch, it will be easier to remove the paper later. Start stitching about two or three stitches before the beginning of the line and end your sewing two or three stitches beyond the line, allowing the stitches to be held in place by the next round of stitching rather than by backstitching.*

Turn the work over and open Piece 2. Finger press the seam open. (**Diagram 14**)

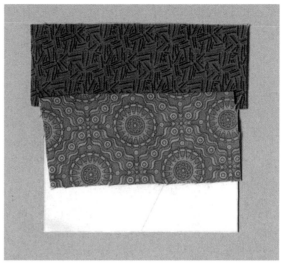

Diagram 14

Turning the work so that the marked side is on top, fold the foundation forward along the line between Space 1+2 and Space 3. Trim about 1/8" to 1/4" from the fold.

It is easier to trim the paper if you pull the paper away from the stitching. If you use fabric as your foundation, fold the fabric forward as far as it will go and then start to trim. (**Diagram 15**)

Diagram 15

Place Fabric #3 right side down even with the just-trimmed edge. (**Diagram 16**)

Diagram 16

Turn the block over to the marked side and sew along the line between Space 1+2 and Space 3. (**Diagram 17**)

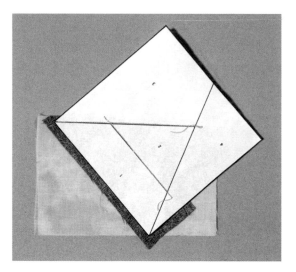

Diagram 17

Turn the work over, open Piece 3 and finger press the seam. (**Diagram 18**)

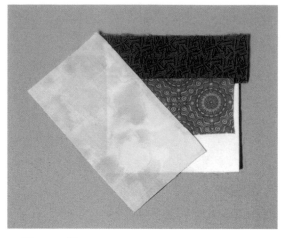

Diagram 18

In the same way you have added the other pieces, add Piece #4 to complete this block. Trim the fabric $^{1}/4$" from the edge of the foundation. The foundation-pieced block is completed. (**Diagram 19**)

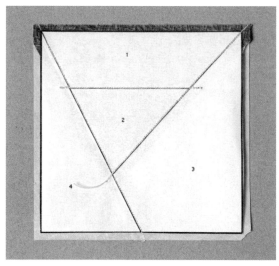

Diagram 19

After you have finished sewing a block, don't immediately remove the paper. Since you are often piecing with tiny bits of fabric, grainline is not a factor. Therefore, some of the pieces may have been cut on the bias and may have a tendency to stretch. You can eliminate any problem with distortion by keeping the paper in place until all of the blocks have been sewn together. If, however, you want to remove the paper, stay stitch along the outer edge of the block to help keep the block in shape.

Sewing Multiple Sections

Many of the blocks in foundation piecing are created with two or more sections. These sections, which are indicated by letters, are individually pieced and then sewn together. The cutting line for these sections is indicated by a red line. Before you start to make any of these multi-section blocks, begin by cutting the foundation piece apart so that each section is worked independently. Leave a 1/4" seam allowance around each section.

Following the instructions beginning on page 116 for Making the Block, complete each section. Then place the sections right side together. Pin the corners of the top section to the corners of the bottom section. (**Diagram 20**)

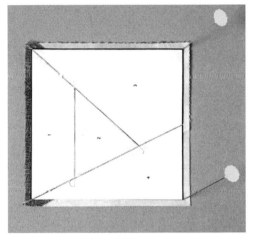

Diagram 20

If you are certain that the pieces are aligned correctly, sew the two sections together using the regular stitch length on the sewing machine.

Press the sections open and continue sewing the sections in pairs. (**Diagram 21**)

Diagram 21

Sew necessary pairs of sections together to complete the block. (**Diagram 22**)

Diagram 22

The blocks are now ready to sew into your quilt.

What You Don't Want to Forget

• If you plan to sew by hand, begin by taking some backstitches that will anchor the thread at the beginning of the line. Then use a backstitch every four of five stitches. End the stitching with a few backstitches.

• If you plan to sew by machine, start stitching two or three stitches before the start of the stitching line and finish your stitching two or three stitches beyond the end.

• Use a short stitch (about 20 stitches per inch) for paper foundations to make it easier to remove the paper. If the paper falls apart as you sew, your stitches are too short.

• Finger press (or use an iron) each seam as you finish it.

• Stitching which goes from a space into another space will not interfere with adding additional fabric pieces.

• Remember to trim all seam allowances at least 1/4".

• When sewing points, start from the wide end and sew towards the point.

• Unless you plan to use it only once in the block, it is a good idea to stay away from directional prints in foundation piecing.

• When cutting pieces for foundation piecing, never worry about the grainline.

• Always remember to sew on the marked side, placing the fabric on the unmarked side,

• Follow the numerical order, or it won't work.

• Once you have finished making a block do not remove the paper until the entire quilt has been finished unless you stay stitch around the outside of the block.

• Be sure that the ink you use to make your foundation is permanent and will not wash out into your fabric.

Templates

Mijochun, page 78, and *Easy Road*, page 26, are made using templates. Acrylic templates in the proper size are now available in many quilt stores, but if you do not have access to acrylic templates, you can easily make templates using the patterns found with the individual instructions. These templates are designed to be used for either machine or hand piecing. If you are planning to piece your block by machine, the template should be cut on the solid line to include the 1/4" seam allowance. If the template is to be used for hand piecing, cut the template on the dotted line and add the 1/4" seam allowance when you cut the fabric.

Trace the template pattern onto tracing paper; then glue the pattern onto your choice of template material. Templates can be made out of heavy cardboard, template plastic, even sandpaper. It is important that the templates be cut out carefully because if they are not accurate, the pieces will not fit together. Use a pair of good scissors (not the scissors that you might plan to use for cutting the fabric), a single-edged razor blade, or a craft knife.

It is important to remember that the constant tracing around a cardboard or sandpaper template may cause the edges to wear so that the pattern pieces may begin to change their shape. Make certain that your template stays

consistent, and be prepared to make new templates when the original ones are no longer accurate.

Curved Piecing

Place a light green A right sides together with blue B matching center points along curved edges. Pin in place at center. (**Diagram 23**)

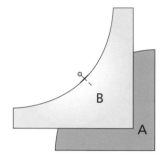

Diagram 23

Place a pin at each end of curve. (**Diagram 24**)

Diagram 24

Sew curved edges being sure B is on top so you can work with raw edges bringing them together as you sew. (**Diagram 25**)

Diagram 25

Press seam toward B. (**Diagram 26**)

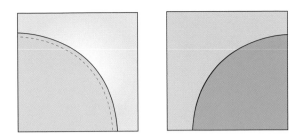

Diagram 26

Finishing Your Quilt

Borders

Borders are usually added to the top, sides and bottom of a quilt.

Simple Borders

To add your borders, measure the quilt top lengthwise and cut two border strips to that length by the width measurement given in the instructions. Strips may have to be pieced to achieve the correct length.

To make the joining seam less noticeable, sew the strips together diagonally. Place two strips right sides together at right angles. Sew a diagonal seam. (**Diagram 27**)

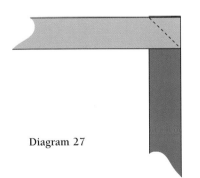

Diagram 27

Trim excess fabric $1/4"$ from stitching. (**Diagram 28**)

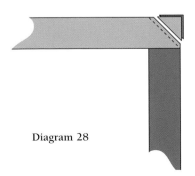

Diagram 28

Press seam open. (**Diagram 29**)

Diagram 29

Sew strips to the sides of the quilt. Now measure the quilt top crosswise, being sure to include the borders you have just added. Cut two border strips to that length, following the width measurement given in the instructions.

Add these borders to the top and bottom of the quilt.

Repeat this process for any additional borders. Use the $1/4"$ seam allowance at all times and press all of the seams toward the border just added. Press the quilt top carefully.

Mitered Borders

Mitered borders are much more time-consuming than simple borders, but the results may well be worth the effort.

Measure the quilt top lengthwise. Cut two strips that length plus twice the finished border width plus $1/2"$ for seam allowances (piece if necessary to achieve the length needed).

Measure the quilt top crosswise. Cut, piecing if necessary, two strips that length plus twice the finished border width plus $1/4"$.

Find the midpoint of one of the side border strips by folding strip in half. (**Diagram 30**)

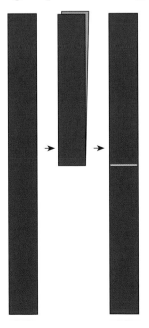

Diagram 30

121

Place strip right sides together with quilt top matching midpoint of border with midpoint of quilt side. Pin in place. (**Diagram 31**)

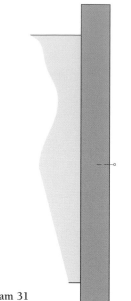

Diagram 31

Pin border to quilt top along entire side. The border strip will extend beyond the quilt top at both ends.

Beginning 1/4" from top edge of quilt top, sew border strip to quilt top, ending 1/4" from bottom edge. Backstitch at beginning and ending of sewing. (**Diagram 32**) Repeat with remaining border strips being careful not to catch extended border strips edges in your sewing.

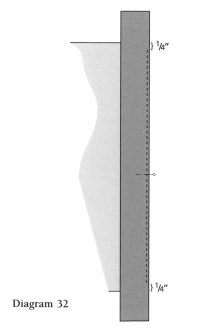

} 1/4"

} 1/4"

Diagram 32

To finish corners fold quilt top in half diagonally; borders will extend straight up and away from quilt.

Place ruler along folded edge of quilt top going into border strip; draw a diagonal line on the border. (**Diagram 33**)

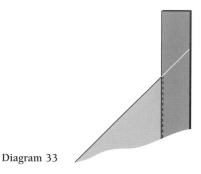

Diagram 33

Beginning at the corner of the quilt top, stitch along drawn line to the edge of the border strip. (**Diagram 34**)

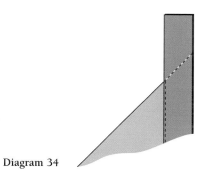

Diagram 34

Open the quilt at corner to check miter. If satisfied, trim excess fabric 1/4" from diagonal seam. (**Diagram 35**)

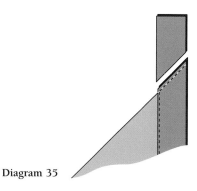

Diagram 35

Repeat process at remaining three corners.

Attaching the Batting and Backing

There are a number of different types of batting on the market today including the new fusible battings that eliminate the need for basting. Your choice of batting will depend upon how you are planning to use your quilt. If the quilt is to serve as a wall hanging, you will probably want to use a thin cotton batting. A quilt made with a thin cotton or cotton/polyester blend works best for machine quilting. Very thick polyester batting should be used only for tied quilts.

It is a good idea to remove the batting from its wrapping 24 hours before you plan to use it and open it out to full size. You will find that the batting will now lie flat when you are ready to use it.

The best fabric for quilt backing is 100% cotton fabric. If your quilt is larger than the available fabric you will have to piece your backing fabric. When joining the fabric, try not to have a seam going down the center. Instead cut off the selvages and make a center strip that is about 36" wide and have narrower strips at the sides. Seam the pieces together and carefully iron the seams open. (This is one of the few times in making a quilt that a seam should be pressed open.) Several fabric manufacturers are now selling fabric in 90" or 108"-widths for use as backing fabric.

The batting and the backing should be cut about one to two inches larger on all sides than the quilt top. Place the backing wrong side up on a flat surface. Smooth out the batting on top of this, matching the outer edges. Center the quilt top, right side up, on top of the batting.

Now the quilt layers must be held together before quilting, and there are several methods for doing this:

Safety-pin Basting: Starting from the center and working toward the edges, pin through all layers at one time with large safety pins. The pins should be placed no more than 4" apart. As you work, think of your quilting plan to make sure that the pins will avoid prospective quilting lines.

Thread Basting: Baste the three layers together with long stitches. Start in the center and sew toward the edges in a number of diagonal lines.

Quilt-gun Basting: This handy trigger tool pushes nylon tags through all layers of the quilt. Start in the center and work toward the outside edges. The tags should be placed about 4" apart. You can sew right over the tags, which can then be easily removed by cutting them off with scissors.

Spray or Heat-set Basting: Several manufacturers have spray adhesives available especially for quilters. Apply these products by following the manufacturers' directions. You might want to test these products before you use them to make sure that they meet your requirements.

Fusible Iron-on Batting: These battings are a wonderful new way to hold quilt layers together without using any of the other time-consuming methods of basting. Again, you will want to test these battings to be certain that you are happy with the results. Follow the manufacturers' directions.

Quilting

If you like the process of hand quilting, you can—of course—finish these projects by hand quilting. However, if you want to finish these quilts quickly, you might want to use a sewing machine for quilting.

If you have never used a sewing machine for quilting, you may want to find a book and read about the technique. You do not need a special machine for quilting. Just make sure that your machine has been oiled and is in good working condition.

If you are going to do machine quilting, you should invest in an even-feed foot. This foot is designed to feed the top and bottom layers of a quilt evenly through the machine. The foot prevents puckers from forming as you machine quilt. Use a fine transparent nylon thread in the top and regular sewing thread in the bobbin.

Quilting in the ditch is one of the easiest ways to machine quilt. This is a term used to describe stitching along the seam line between two pieces of fabric. Using your fingers, pull the blocks or pieces apart slightly and machine stitch right between the two pieces. The stitching will look better if you keep the stitching to the side of the seam that does not have the extra bulk of the seam allowance under it. The quilting will be hidden in the seam.

Free-form machine quilting can be used to quilt around a design or to quilt a motif. The quilting is done with a darning foot and the feed dogs down on the sewing machine. It takes practice to master Free-form quilting because you are controlling the movement of the quilt under the needle rather than the sewing machine moving the quilt. You can quilt in any direction—up and down, side-to-side and even in circles—without pivoting the quilt around the needle. Practice this quilting method before trying it on your quilt.

Making Bias Strips

Sometimes you will need to use bias strips to finish a project, for example, binding the edges of Through My Garden Window, page 132. Bias strips are used when you need to go around curved edges.

To make the strips, you need to start out with a square of fabric. For smaller quilts, you will need a square that is at least 18" x 18". You will get about 90" of $2^{1}/2$"-wide bias strips from an 18" square. A 24" square will make about 120" of $2^{1}/2$"-wide bias strips.

Using a ruler and a fabric marking pencil, draw 45-degree diagonal lines across the square. (**Diagram 36**) It is important that the lines are at a 45 degree angle to achieve strips that are along the true bias.

Diagram 36

Cut along the drawn lines. (**Diagram 37**)

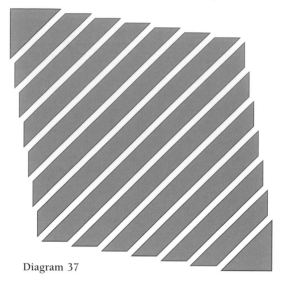

Diagram 37

Place two strips right sides together at a right angle. Slide ends so that small triangles are formed that extend about $1/2$" from each end. (**Diagram 38**) Pin in place.

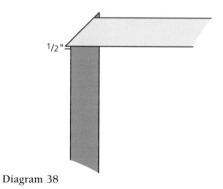

1/2"

Diagram 38

Sew strips together beginning and ending where strips intersect. (**Diagram 39**) Press seam open.

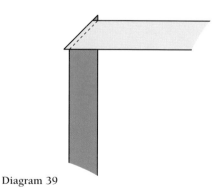

Diagram 39

Continue sewing strips together until desired length is achieved.

Attaching the Continuous Machine Binding

Once the quilt has been quilted, the edges must be bound. Start by trimming the backing and batting even with the quilt top. Measure the quilt top and cut enough 2$^1/2$"-wide strips to go around all four sides of the quilt plus 12". Join the strips end to end with diagonal seams and trim the corners. Press the seams open. (**Diagram 40**)

Diagram 40

Cut one end of the strip at a 45-degree angle and press under $^1/4$". (**Diagram 41**)

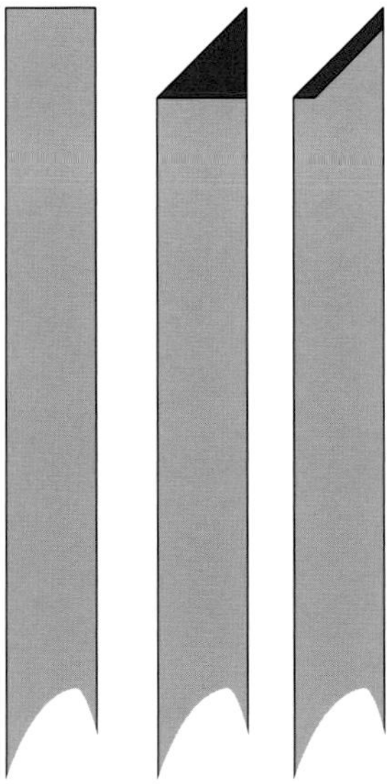

Diagram 41

Press entire strip in half lengthwise, wrong sides together. (**Diagram 42**)

Diagram 42

On the back of the quilt, position the binding in the middle of one side, keeping the raw edges together. Sew the binding to the quilt with the $^1/4$" seam allowance, beginning about three inches below the folded end of the binding. (**Diagram 43**)

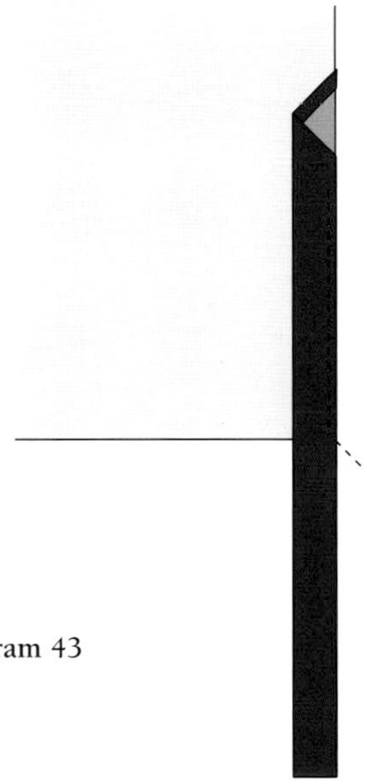

Diagram 43

At the corner, stop $^1/4$" from the edge of the quilt and backstitch.

Fold binding away from quilt so it is at a right angle to edge just sewn. Then, fold the binding back on itself so the fold is on the quilt edge and the raw edges are aligned with the adjacent side of the quilt. Begin sewing at the quilt edge. (**Diagram 44**)

Diagram 44

Continue in the same way around the remaining sides of the quilt. Stop about 2" away from the starting point. Trim any excess binding and tuck it inside the folded end. Finish the stitching. (**Diagram 45**)

Diagram 45

Fold the binding to the front of the quilt so the seam line is covered; machine-stitch the binding in place on the front of the quilt. Use a straight stitch or tiny zigzag with invisible or matching thread. If you have a sewing machine that does embroidery stitches, you may want to use your favorite stitch.

Adding a Rod Pocket

In order to hang your quilt for family and friends to enjoy, you will need to attach a rod pocket to the back.

Cut a strip of fabric, 6" wide by the width of the quilt.

Fold short ends of strip under $1/4$", then fold another $1/4$". Sew along first fold. (**Diagram 46**)

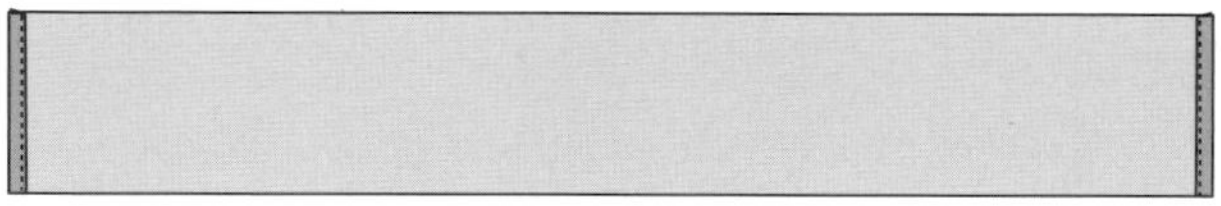

Diagram 46

Fold strip lengthwise with wrong sides together. Sew along raw edges with a $1/4$" seam allowance to form a long tube. (**Diagram 47**)

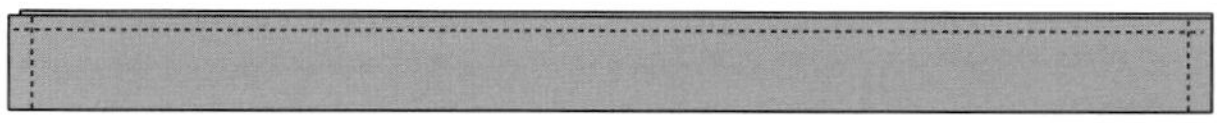

Diagram 47

Place tube on ironing surface with seam up and centered; press seam open and folds flat. (**Diagram 48**)

Diagram 48

Place tube on back of quilt, seam side against quilt, about 1" from top edge and equal distant from side edges. (**Diagram 49**) Pin in place so tube is straight across quilt.

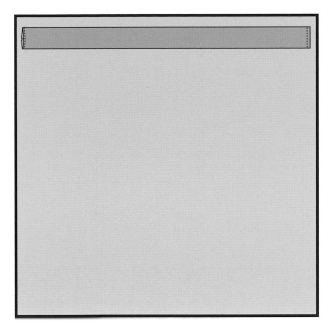

Diagram 49

Hand stitch top and bottom edges of tube to back of quilt being careful not to let stitches show on front of quilt.

Labeling Your Quilt

Always sign and date your quilt when finished. You can make a label by cross-stitching or embroidering or even writing on a label or on the back of your quilt with a permanent marking pen. If you are friends with your computer, you can even create an attractive label on the computer.

Metric Equivalents

inches	cm	inches	cm	inches	cm
1	2.54	11	27.94	21	53.34
2	5.08	12	30.48	22	55.88
3	7.62	13	33.02	23	58.42
4	10.16	14	35.56	24	60.96
5	12.70	15	38.10	30	76.20
6	15.24	16	40.64	36	91.44
7	17.78	17	43.18	42	106.68
8	20.32	18	45.72	48	121.92
9	22.86	19	48.26	54	137.16
10	25.40	20	50.80	60	152.40

Index